Rev ⬆Up!

BOLD AND DISRUPTIVE STRATEGIES

TO **Rev ⬆p!**

YOUR REVENUE CYCLE
HERO'S JOURNEY

JAYSON YARDLEY

www.revupbook.com
jayson@yardleyinc.com

Rev Up! / Jayson Yardley.—1st ed.
Soft Cover Edition ISBN 978-1-7337733-0-0
Ebook ISBN 978-1-7337733-1-7

Dedication

*Dedicated to my amazing wife Holly and
incredible kids Will and Brianna.*

To Ryan Skye Yardley, I miss you and think of you daily.

To my parents Rich and Val.

*To all my supportive and loving family: Barbara, Chuck,
Martha, Sissy, Jill, Judy, Margaret, Andi, Dani, Audra,
Ashley, Tyler, Matt, Kevin, Michael F., Michael J., Jim, Tova,
Scott, Janice, David, Jocelyn, Cheryl, Rick, and Chris.*

*To my loving Upstate New York family,
Donna, Katy, Clare, and Gabor.*

*To our new Jones family, thank you for accepting Holly and
all of us into your lives. Commander Eric Jones and
Lorena Jones, we love you. To our new brother and sister,
Rick & Erica, it's a better life with you as our new siblings.*

Acknowledgments

I'd like to thank the many healthcare leaders and revenue cycle professionals who have inspired me throughout my career in healthcare. The countless lessons of empathy, service, leadership, empowerment, and going beyond status quo to positively and boldly impact the experiences patients, families, and the broader healthcare ecosystem deserve have enriched, challenged and brought purpose to my vocation.

Hats off to the generous contributors to this book who willingly shared of themselves, their stories, and healthcare experiences. You are all heroes who aspire to improve healthcare and the patient financial experience in all that you do. Many thanks to Bradley Tinnermon, Jessica Cole, Dave Muhs, Chris Johnson, Mike Allen, and Deborah Vancleave.

To Micah Solomon, your help has been invaluable and wisdom about customer experience surefire.

To Christine Hanson-Ehlinger and Karen Sandrick, whose brilliant advice contributed greatly in inspiring and completing this book. Your professionalism and skills are unrivaled, thank you. And, to the extended Avadyne Health family, it's a pleasure to see how all of you are champions of the patient financial experience and provide so much value to so many every day.

Finally, to my immediate and extended family, thank you for your unwavering encouragement and joy daily. My incredible wife, Holly, and children, Will and Brianna, bring inspiration, strength, love, and purpose to every day.

And to Rich and Val Yardley, my parents, your lifelong guidance and superhero ways were beyond generous and impactful. I am forever grateful.

Contents

Preface

When I look around me, I know I'm lucky to be surrounded by superheroes every day. This book is an attempt for me to help these everyday superheroes and is dedicated to the original superheroes in my life…my parents.

All through my life, my parents were loving, hard-working, perfectly imperfect people who provided wonderful examples for me. As healthcare professionals, they did not save lives in the operating room, but they figured out how to keep hospital doors open and MRIs humming through the management of the business side of healthcare. Ultimately, I would follow in their footsteps, secure in their healthcare shadow, and then break out to forge my own path.

For most of his career, my dad was a hospital CFO. During my high school years, he was CFO at the local community hospital. I'll always remember a fateful Christmas when nurses ran my father and me off of a floor of the hospital. Apparently handing out cookies to patients with diabetes and strict dietary restrictions was frowned upon at that institution. I learned much from him about managing people and handling difficult discussions and situations.

My mom was a business office director in a downtown Los Angeles hospital. She and her team worked in a dungeon of a basement. She worked crazy hours and sacrificed much of her time so she could complete the sixty-mile drive before traffic and return home during the first wave of the gridlock. One summer as a teenager, I joined her during my vacation to "discharge" patients from the hospital's computer systems. I remember asking why we had to "discharge" the patients in the computer when they had already gone home. She grinned and provided her response looking at me over the top of her glasses and repeating the series of function keys I needed to enter to discharge the patients. Looking back down at the ruler sitting on the green-bar paper list of patients to be discharged, I mumbled under my breath that the hospital could at least upgrade to a state-of-the-art computer system like my Commodore 64.

Other summer breaks, my parents would take me to healthcare industry conventions in Palm Springs, California. I'd see many of their professional friends, there were parties every night, and reportedly they attended classes or meetings during the day. I'm not sure about the meetings, but I now know that taking a teenage boy to healthcare industry conventions during his summer vacation was some form of child abuse. Abuse or not, healthcare was finding its way into my blood.

Fast-forward over thirty years to the time when I was a healthcare executive trying to care for my sick father.

Most of us begin and end our lives at a hospital. My father was no exclusion to this rule. His final trip to the hospital would be the result of stage 4 prostate cancer. That morning had started like most of the mornings over the past few weeks. My wife got up early to check on my dad. He was a mile from our house at a medical nursing home. As he became sicker as his cancer spread throughout his body, his care had become too much for us to maintain at our house. I hated taking him to a nursing home, but even I struggled to hold him as he transitioned from bed to wheelchair to chair to bathroom and back.

That morning my dad was having trouble catching his breath. The nursing home doctor didn't like how he sounded and my wife demanded they call an ambulance. She reached out to me and I arrived just before the ambulance. The paramedics whisked my dad away and I followed them to the hospital, which was luckily only a few blocks away.

I'll never forget the next series of events. My father was taken by the paramedics through the hospital's ambulance entrance to the emergency room. I parked my car and headed through the main emergency room doors. I explained to the volunteer who I was and she opened the doors to allow me back to the clinical area of the emergency room. I walked down a hallway of open bay emergency rooms on either side and rounded a nurse's desk area to find a physician and what felt like an army of nurses standing with him. I heard a paramedic inform the physician, "That's his son."

The physician introduced himself and shook my hand. In that moment I knew it was serious. Everyone else stopped talking and just looked at me. I can't explain their look other than they all looked at me with a level of sadness in their eyes.

The physician was direct, yet kind in his words. "I'm sorry to tell you that your father's organs and systems are failing. The only way to keep him alive is to place him on life support. I understand that is not his wish. According to his Durable Power of Attorney, you need to tell me how you would like to proceed. We can place him on life support or we can make him comfortable in the amount of time he has left with us. I can't tell you how long that will be."

Somehow I answered the doctor through a clenched jaw. It was the only way I could speak without bursting into tears. "My father's wishes were clear. He did not want to be on life support. But I promised my sister I would not make this decision alone. Can I quickly call her?"

In a few moments, I had spoken to my sister who agreed with my response. I returned to the doctor, tears in my eyes, and confirmed that my dad would not want to be on life support. He acknowledged me and quietly uttered instructions to the nursing staff. They flew into action.

The doctor turned to me and told me and my wife (who had now joined me) to go be with my dad. Take as much time as we needed. He didn't know how long that would be. They would not move my dad and they would not disturb us, unless we needed something. I placed calls to the immediate family to tell them the news. My aunts and stepmom were on the way.

It didn't take long. My wife and I each held one of my dad's hands. We talked to him and his breath labored. Over time, he calmed, then slowed, and stopped. Maybe one tearful hour had passed.

In that time, I lost one of my superheroes. I loved my dad and mom. My superheroes.

A few weeks passed and what came next changed my career focus. What came next was a mountain of patient statements, Explanations of Benefits (EOBs), and various materials from healthcare providers, insurance companies, and others. I found myself thinking—I've been in healthcare revenue cycle for over twenty years, for my entire life as I remember back to those summers of healthcare conferences. If I'm struggling to figure this out, how in the world can a nonhealthcare professional do it?

For over twenty years, I had worked IN healthcare revenue cycle. My motivation had now changed to work ON healthcare revenue cycle and the complicated industry, processes, and technologies that create mountains of frustrations at a time when patients (and some-times grieving sons) want simplification. My goal was to find ways that would create a better, empowered Patient Financial Experience. It was this passion and pursuit that drove me to take the position of CEO at Avadyne Health. At Avadyne, I found an organization that was equally focused on the Patient Financial Experience.

I quickly realized that in order to improve the Patient Financial Experience, I needed to focus on the people most directly responsible for it: healthcare revenue cycle leaders, Chief Financial Officers, and those many wonderful people who work within the revenue cycles of hospitals and health systems across the country. The revenue cycle superheroes who can be found in the basements and off-site locations at every hospital in America. These are not people with comic book super-abilities of flight or immortality, but the ones who have the most super-abilities of all—grit, compassion, character, and a purpose-driven approach to helping patients.

In the pursuit of supporting these heroes came the idea for this book. In this book, I hope that I help, in some small way, the hero's journey of revenue cycle and healthcare leaders across the country.

Introduction

In my opinion, the portion of the healthcare revenue cycle business focused on communicating and collecting patient liabilities has not changed markedly for twenty-five years. The revenue cycle sends out a bill that shows what the patient owes and does some collection around it through letter campaigns and call centers that allow patients to phone in and ask questions or make payments.

Over the last couple of years there has been a push toward self-service options that diminish the necessity for the call center and financing that offers extended payment plans or loans to patients.

But the shift to self-service has not been an easy one. Consumers are used to self-service when it comes to travel or banking or other online purchasing; they know what they're buying and how much it is going to cost. Healthcare by its very nature is confusing; there are multiple hands in the pot—insurers as well as providers—that affect the price of a service and the amount owed. The experience is far different. Think how a consumer would feel if she bought an airline ticket and then learned at check-in that the price she paid was only an estimate; she stills owes a thousand dollars.

Technological advances in the form of telephone dialers, integrated voice recognition, and rudimentary online payment capabilities have just brushed the surface. The revenue cycle business is missing something fundamental: how to understand patients as consumers of healthcare services and how to relate to them as such. Today's revenue cycle leaders struggle to get data about patient satisfaction and other analytics and meet the expectations of hospital boards and their leadership teams to provide a better patient financial experience.

Revenue cycle leaders are in a challenged place, whether or not they recognize it. The business model is changing, the patient is the new payer, and healthcare is far more complicated than anything else a patient spends money on. The cost providers pay to collect patient balances is rising no matter whether payment comes in on day one or day 120, whether a patient received one statement or three, whether a patient paid online or by check or had to speak with a revenue cycle representative one time or ten.

In some respects revenue cycle leaders are being asked to accomplish the impossible, at least in the universe of today: provide a better patient experience at lower cost while driving higher collections. Revenue cycle leaders need a new way of looking at where they are now and where they need to be. It is a journey one could liken to that of a hero, as described by Joseph Campbell.

Joseph Campbell was a professor of literature at Sarah Lawrence College. In his lifelong research of hero myths and stories from around the world, Campbell discovered common patterns that he codified as the Hero's Journey or the stages almost every quest goes through, no matter the culture or the myth.

As described by Campbell, the Hero's Journey begins in the Ordinary World. This world is ordinary to those who live there but it has characteristics that are troubling. For heroes to begin their journey, they must be called away by a discovery, or an event, that makes them realize the problems that beset their world. After accepting the Call to Adventure, the hero enters an outside world with its own rules, confronts a series of obstacles, gains help from tools and helpers, and ends up changing the ordinary.

You'll learn more about the Hero's Journey in storytelling and Joseph Campbell in Chapter One. Let me just say here that revenue cycle leaders are on the threshold of a hero's journey in healthcare. Hospitals are getting distress signals in the form of uncollected accounts, rising bad debt, and surging patient complaints. Obstacles in the form of villains are threatening hospitals. Their weapons? Complaints, dissatisfaction, increasing cost to collect, slow payment of outstanding account balances, and ineffective training and tools. The ultimate blow: sabotaged patient loyalty, with lost revenue for years to come.

The Ordinary World for revenue cycle leaders appears to be stuck in somewhat of a time warp at most hospitals, with outdated tools and practices driving dissatisfaction. Even with entire hospital committees devoted to improving the Patient Experience, investments in the financial side of the experience are often lacking.

It's the revenue cycle leaders of today who can rise to the occasion and accept the Call to Action. No one else better understands the need to fully embrace innovation and offer patients more modern, empowered, financial experiences and services. A piecemeal approach—a new payment portal or a more attractive hospital bill—is not enough. Neither is mere discussion, or debate, without leading to real change. Action is needed at this critical juncture, both in terms of changing mind-set and making actual investments. It's the right thing to do for patients, millions of whom are struggling with higher-than-ever out-of-pocket costs, and to respond to the changing healthcare marketplace, consumer behavior, regulations, and insurance. All these developments are happening in tandem. They're all pointing in the same direction. Standing still, rejecting the Call to Action, is not the answer. It's time to modernize and "consumerize" the financial care hospitals provide to patients.

However, all innovations require a roadmap. That's where this book comes in. Chapter by chapter, I'll cover the components of the financial experience. We'll look at how price estimates need to be done, why patients need multiple options to pay their bills, how new technologies can help answer questions about patient liability, and what kinds of new models can be put in place to control the cost to collect. We'll also look closely at why the financial experience needs to be scored for real-time resolution and continuous quality improvement.

In addition to my zest for revenue cycle, I also enjoy pop culture. In each chapter, I reference pop culture movies and stories to help illustrate concepts of the Hero's Journey. At the end of each chapter, I'll provide a few questions for you to consider on your journey and to frame the direction the journey may take. As Peter Drucker, the father of modern management put it, "The most serious mistakes are not being made as a result of wrong answers. The truly dangerous thing is asking the wrong questions."

As you can tell, I'm pretty passionate when it comes to reshaping the Patient Financial Experience. That's because I've seen positive changes occur once hospitals really give it the respect—and the resources—it deserves. Changing the Ordinary World of the financial experience calls for analytics to measure satisfaction and specialized training for revenue cycle employees. It means delivering bills by email or text instead of only traditional mail methods, communicating with patients via chat and apps, and reframing collection as a concierge experience. Internal market study data indicate that the financial experience patients want includes not one, but all of those components.

The benefits of this transformation go way beyond resolution of individual patient accounts. Consider the amount of revenue gained from an account that's paid in full. Then factor in the costs that are saved because it doesn't go to collection or because better patient engagement tools decreased the overall cost to collect. Add in the intangible amount of future revenue from the patient, the patient's family and friends, and others who choose your hospital because of the financial care you're known for. Now you're starting to see the true impact of the holistic Patient Financial Experience.

It's time to be innovative, insightful, and strategic. It's time to step beyond the borders of what's known and embrace change (in a calculated way, of course, since the benefits are fully supported by data!). In this book, I'll demonstrate how a new approach to the Patient Financial Experience turns some of the revenue cycle's biggest pain points into opportunities for differentiation.

I know that it's possible for any hospital to put the right pieces in place. I've seen it happen, and at those hospitals, leadership doesn't see the Patient Financial Experience as a source of angst. It is a time, and an unprecedented one, for the revenue cycle to assert itself as a change maker. For the hospital, it's an exciting way to differentiate itself from competitors that rely on outdated processes and hope to somehow get different results.

We started with a whole host of manual processes and gradually moved to technology, and third-party services to become more state-of-the-art. Beginning at ground zero, in twenty-four months we've been able to cut our final denial write-offs in half. This equates to millions of dollars saved. We've also been able to bring quality registration and patient satisfaction to the forefront. We have been sharing data with our service line leaders on a monthly basis and patient complaints are down nearly 75 percent.

Deborah Vancleave, Vice President of
Revenue Cycle, Mosaic Life Care

The revenue cycle knows change is needed. Revenue cycle leaders see the gaps, the inconsistencies, and the dissatisfaction that come from obsolete and fragmented processes. What typically hasn't been tried is a look at the process as a whole, instead of separate pieces that need fixing.

Each chapter of this book covers a different "piece" of the financial satisfaction picture. You'll notice that the chapters have a hero/villain theme. That's my way of underscoring the magnitude and excitement of the opportunity for the revenue cycle at this juncture. It's also a Call to Action and a series of steps that fit together to form a Revenue Cycle Hero's Journey. As each of these pieces falls into place, a truly holistic Patient Financial Experience will gradually appear. Your hospital will then be in an excellent position to become a hero to patients, gaining loyalty while at the same time controlling costs. We'll carefully examine just what it means for hospitals to be the first in their marketplace to offer a premiere Patient Financial Experience to everyone who comes to their doors. In my eyes, that's something pretty heroic.

We'll explore the true toll of the revenue cycle obstacles or "villains" on hospitals, yes. But just like any myth, we'll conclude with a look at a New World and what it does for the Patient Financial Experience as well as the hospital's bottom line. With that, I invite you to turn the page and reconsider everything you've come to assume about the Patient Financial Experience...and find out just what it takes to become a Revenue Cycle Hero.

CHAPTER 1

The Revenue Cycle Hero's Journey

Heroes, particularly super ones, are central to our popular culture. Heroes drive attendance for the highest grossing motion pictures. *Avatar*, at $2.7 billon, leads overall boxoffice sales. Not far behind are *Star Wars: The Force Awakens* and *Avengers: Infinity War* ($2 billion), and *Black Panther* ($1.3 billion). (1)

They fuel book sales. The Harry Potter series has sold 400 million copies worldwide and been translated into 68 languages. Hero Harry has not lost his luster. 2016's *Harry Potter and the Cursed Child* was the best-selling book for the year. *The Hunger Games*, featuring Katniss Everdeen, has the highest digital sales for adults or children. (2)

Heroes are prominent in video games—the top characters are Doom Slayer, Kratus (God of War), Mega Man, and Lara Croft, Tomb Raider, accounting for more than $29 billion worldwide—and television series: *Agents of S.H.I.E.L.D.* and *Supergirl* are returning season after season. (3)

Why Do We Need Heroes?

Philosophers and others say heroes resonate because they lift the spirit, inspire, nourish and strengthen, and demonstrate how to vault over hurdles to transform the world.

In folklore, heroes are superhuman or divine; they have a mystical origin and an unusual strength or ability. But even in mythology some heroes are not invincible; they are known for their willingness to pursue a distant goal, and not always along a direct or clear path; confront whatever lies ahead, be it danger, loneliness, or temptation; marshal friends and accomplices, tools and talismans, and guides; traverse the present darkness and fashion a new, brighter universe or future.

In real life leaders may not consider themselves to be heroes despite their accomplishments and leadership qualities. Mythological and real heroes share many qualities: the courage to confront roadblocks, the virtuosity to act judiciously, not audaciously, and recognize opportunity, determination, focus, compassion, understanding, perseverance, honesty, loyalty, conviction, and fortitude. Few leaders have all these characteristics, but they are responsible and wise enough to identify and nurture the qualities of heroes in others. Real-life heroes listen, do their homework, and ask smart questions.

While real-life heroes do not have abilities far beyond those of mortal men, they nonetheless often follow the same path their mythic counterparts do: facing challenges or combating adversity with integrity, bravery, and fortitude. These heroes demonstrate excellence, are not content with the status quo, stand out, accomplish the extraordinary, and serve as role models.

The Hero's Journey—Its Creator

The Hero's Journey is based on the theory that all folk tales, as well as myths, are variations of a single great story. It came from observations by literature professor and mythologist Joseph Campbell that a common pattern can be found in most great myths, regardless of where they came from or when they were created.

Joseph Campbell was born in 1904 in a suburb of New York City. The child of an Irish immigrant family, Campbell was immersed early in rituals and symbols of the Catholic Church. He became interested in mythology when he saw Native Americans in Buffalo Bill's Wild West Show in Madison Square Garden. Over the years he continued to study Native American lore as well as Indian exhibits at the American Museum of Natural History. Campbell also studied Arthurian legends, the psychological theories of Sigmund Freud and Karl Jung, and the myths in Thomas Mann's novels. (5)

Campbell's *The Hero of a Thousand Faces*, published in 1949, introduced the notion that hero stories involving Buddha, Krishna, and Moses have the same basis in mythology, introduced the concept of the Hero's Journey to the public, explained how ancient stories were connected to modern life and how challenges lead individuals on an adventure that follows the same trajectory whether the stories are part of literature, myth, ritual, or religion. (6)

In one of the most popular TV series in the history of public television, Campbell discussed the classic hero cycle with Bill Moyers in 1988. The six-part *The Power of Myth* showed how myths of ancient times and the characters they portray influence modern-day beliefs and actions as well as storytelling by writers/producers/directors such as George Lucas. (7)

The Hero's Journey—Its Stages

The Hero's Journey is the story of the man or woman who, through great suffering, explores the core mysteries of their world and finds or develops powers that can free society from the bonds that entangle it. Present in the first stories told by man, the Hero's Journey spread from place to place and evolved over time, taking on characteristics that were more specific to a particular culture or locale along the way. The basic structure remains the same, however.

In myth, legend, and popular storytelling, the Hero's Journey has four parts and twelve steps:

Part One: Call to Adventure
- Step One: The Ordinary World
- Step Two: The Call
- Step Three: Refusal

Part Two: Initiation
- Step Four: The Mentor's Help
- Step Five: The Threshold
- Step Six: Tests

Part Three: Transformation
- Step Seven: Approach
- Step Eight: Ordeal
- Step Nine: Reward

Part Four: The Road Back/The Hero's Return
- Step Ten: The Road Back
- Step Eleven: Atonement
- Step Twelve: Return (8)

The same pattern that can be seen in epic journeys of Moses and Buddha appears in popular culture. Helen Kantilaftis of the New York Film School pointed to five blockbuster films that follow the Hero's Journey. In a post on May 14, 2015, she wrote about: *The Matrix*, *Men in Black*, *The Hunger Games*, *The Lion King*, and *Star Wars*. (9)

Heroes in Business

Many recognize that leadership always is somewhat heroic, in that leaders stand apart, direct, and promote change. David Wilkins in a July 24, 2012 article in *Forbes Magazine* singled out and labeled a number of business leaders as heroes:

- Jeff Bezos of Amazon, as a pioneer in internet commerce
- Ann Mulcahy, a financial turnaround guru at Xerox
- Brad Smith, the innovator behind Intuit and QuickBooks financial software
- Indra Noyi, the one who took PepsiCo in a new healthy food direction
- Howard Schultz, the up-from-the-bootstraps role model from Starbucks (10)

Some of the best books on leadership for 2017 and 2018 have hero themes:

- *The Captain's Class: The Hidden Force that Creates the World's Greatest Teams*, by *Wall Street Journal* editor Sam Walker, explains that winning sports teams have one factor in common: a phenomenal athlete and captain who not only had stellar physical skills but also was dogged, took on thankless jobs, communicated well with and motivated teammates, and stood apart. (11)
- *One Mission: How Leaders Build a Team of Teams* by Charles Fussell tells how U. S. Army General Stanley McChrystal led troops in the Afghanistan war through processes, practice, and traditions that eliminated operational silos and capitalized on real-time information technology and spurred change in business at Intuit and

government in the Oklahoma Office of Management and Enterprise Services. (12)

- *The Startup Hero's Pledge.* Billionaire investor and venture capitalist Tim Draper tells stories about companies such as Skype and Hotmail, providing lessons about setting goals and giving others the freedom to pursue them. (13)

Business Leaders on a Hero's Journey

Authors on leadership take the hero myth with a grain of salt. Greg Satell, author of *Mapping Innovation*, noted that "great leaders aren't heroes, but they can inspire and empower others to be. They create a clear sense of mission, allow people to make their own mistakes and help them to get up when they've been knocked down. They not only point the way forward, they create a visceral desire to get there." (14)

Les McKeown, CEO of Consulting by Predictable Success, warns that leaders can't be heroes 100 percent of the time. "Busting through walls barehanded is exciting to watch, and sometimes required, but at some point, it becomes more effective to simply install a door. Building myths and legends through heroic leadership is a vitally important part of the growth of any business, but insisting on, or regularly depending on mythical, legendary solutions in a complex organization will cap its growth," he wrote. (15)

In his 2013 book *Leadership as a Hero's Journey*, Eric Kaufmann wrote: "When I ask leaders to name a hero, Superman often comes up. Well, Superman…has superhuman powers. He is a perfect being and knows no fear. By contrast, every leader I've met possesses no superhuman powers, is flawed and complex, and is caught in anxiety and fear at new turns (even the existing ones)….It is precisely because of our flawed and anxious nature that we can be heroic. A hero is someone who aims high, makes sacrifices, and gives back. If your leadership is striving for a significant prize, or you find yourself in peril, and you are serving the greater good, then you are poised for the hero's journey." (16)

The Hero's Journey nevertheless has been adapted for business leaders as a way to tell their leadership stories. Kathryn D. Cramer, PhD, founder and managing partner of The Cramer Institute, a leadership consulting and development group based in St. Louis, Missouri, lists six stages of the Hero's Journey: (1) The Call to Action—the time when the hero realizes the need for change; (2) The Resistance—the problems that hold the hero back; (3) The Threshold—the steps the hero takes away from the status quo and beyond business as usual; (4) The Journey—the tests and challenges the hero faces, the villains the hero must confront, the friends the hero can rely upon; (5) The Ordeal—the circumstances that threaten the path the hero has chosen; and (6) The Return Home—the experience, tools, "treasures" the hero brings back to counteract the difficulties and alter The Ordinary World. As Cramer points out, leaders follow the Hero's Journey not because they suffer from hubris, but because they are the instigators of the journey. They will involve others along the way, but they are the ones who heard the Call to Action first. (17)

The Hero's Journey—in the Revenue Cycle

This book adapts Cramer's Hero's Journey for business leaders to the revenue cycle. Its Hero's Journey has seven stages:

1. The Ordinary World. The everyday life of the hero, the leaders of the revenue cycle and C-suite, and all the difficulties they encounter.

2. The Call to Action. The realization that there must be a better way.

3. The Resistance. The bottlenecks and ingrained ways of thinking that get in the way.

4. The Threshold. First steps on the road to an improved revenue cycle.

5. The Journey. The villains and the heroes that confront them.

6. The Transformation. Finding and using cutting-edge tools.

7. The New World of the Patient Financial Experience.

When it comes to financial experiences, the revenue cycle already knows that the Ordinary World—business as usual—is not working for patients. Avadyne Health's recent market research and report confirmed that most patients are unhappy with the financial experience they're getting from hospitals. The Ordinary World is not working for hospitals, either, as they face narrowing margins and increasingly competitive marketplaces. Both hospitals and patients are unhappy with the status quo. But this is not a tragedy; it's an opening. Imagine being the revenue cycle professional who helps a hospital find a way to transform dissatisfied patients into satisfied ones!

For those who are primarily interested in short-term return on investment, good financial care is a proven winner. Metrics shift in a positive direction—not just satisfaction, but also Accounts Receivable (A/R) days, upfront account resolution, bad debt, and more. But that's too narrow a focus when it comes to deciding how much to invest in the Patient Financial Experience. There's actually a much bigger picture to all of this. The ultimate goal is to insulate the hospital financially, allowing it to weather the storm while competitors teeter. Good financial care, it turns out, protects long-term revenue for many years to come. Increasing evidence shows that financial satisfaction drives consumer loyalty. Improved margins in the near term do come along with that, yes. But a more strategic focus, with an eye to the future, is also essential.

As CFO, if I get involved in the Patient Experience, it's usually because someone is upset about their bill or the way they were treated by revenue cycle staff. A couple of years ago after we did a few initiatives to enhance the Patient Financial Experience, an acquaintance said to me: "Dave, I really like what you did in the front lobby. My son had surgery this morning and we have a high-deductible health plan. Your admission staff helped us through everything: how much it would cost and what the estimate would be, and then gave us options for payment. I was so stressed about how to pay for this. Now that stress is gone and I can focus on my son."

Dave Muhs, Chief Financial Officer,
Henry County Health Center

The Ordinary World is changing. Hospital billing, account resolution and collection practices, and cost containment efforts must be based on modern consumer preferences and behavior. New technology and new communication options provide a much needed jolt to routine financial practices—but only if they're implemented. The idea is for hospitals to actually engage patients based on their individual needs, as opposed to a cost prohibitive, one-size-fits-all model. How would this look to a typical hospital patient? Imagine augmented reality avatars explaining a hospital bill, while your best, highly-trained representatives are having complex conversations on high-dollar self-pay liabilities. (And that's just the beginning!)

No clinical team would ignore evidence-based guidelines that are known to improve patient care. Similarly, no revenue cycle leader can afford to disregard the growing body of evidence surrounding financial care. These smart, cost-effective models are proven satisfiers for patients and money-savers for the hospital. And the entire financial experience must be considered in its entirety. Hospital patients are having not one, but multiple financial encounters. They all have to be positive, in order to drive satisfaction. A holistic approach, from price estimates to account resolution, is the only way to ensure the financial experience is world-class…from the very first encounter to the last.

We've all heard a lot about how hospitals are all one step away from financial disaster due to healthcare consumerism. If you want to read more dire warnings, this is not the book for you. I'll certainly be putting bad financial care under the microscope. I'm going to take a close look at financial encounters both from the hospital's point of view, and the patient's. I'll contrast what great financial care looks like compared to the outdated, dissatisfying encounters patients are experiencing.

But the point of this book is not to dwell on the negative. It's not a cautionary tale about what's at stake if hospitals don't get the Patient Financial Experience right. Hospitals already know the cost—they live it every day. What the revenue cycle needs most—and what this book is really all about—is a change in attitude. It's a forward-looking vision of "If we embrace innovation, patient financial satisfaction will follow" that will transform financial care as we know it. From that standpoint, the necessary investments will follow to lead the hospital from the Call to Action to The New World.

Questions & Considerations

- Are you already on a hero's journey? What initiatives or changes are you currently implementing in your revenue cycle or healthcare setting?

- Who are the supporters, guides, and helpers you can rely upon to assist you in your journey?
- What are the priorities for your health system or hospital? How do the following play a role in those priorities?
  - Patient Experience
  - Cost controls or reductions
  - Cash collections
- What is the current state of your Patient Financial Experience?
- Do you take a holistic or siloed approach to the revenue cycle and the Patient Financial Experience?

CHAPTER 2

The Ordinary Revenue Cycle World

After a government agency makes first contact with alien life forms in 1961, alien refugees begin living in secret on Earth, mostly disguised as humans in the New York metropolitan area. A covert agency, known as the Men in Black (MiB), polices these aliens, protects Earth from intergalactic threats, and uses memory-erasing neuralyzers to keep alien activity hidden. Agents have their former identities erased, and retired agents are neuralyzed and given new identities. After an operation to arrest an alien criminal near the Mexican border by Agents Kay and Dee, Agent Dee decides that he is too old for this job. Agent Kay neuralyzes him and recruits a new partner: Agent Jay.

> **Agent Kay:** All right, kid, here's the deal. At any given time there are approximately 1,500 aliens on the planet, most of them right here in Manhattan. And most of them are decent enough; they're just trying to make a living.

Agent Jay: Cab drivers?

Agent Kay: Not as many as you'd think.
Men in Black, Columbia Pictures, 1997

In the hero's journey of myth and motion pictures, the Ordinary World represents the hero's everyday life. It provides context, a home base, and background, and although it may appear to be mundane and calm, it is unstable. The Ordinary World harbors seeds of change that hunger for growth. In *Men in Black*, the Ordinary World is not what appears to New Yorkers, and that's the way MiB wants it.

> **Agent Jay:** I don't know whether or not you've forgotten, but there's an Arquillian Battle Cruiser that's about to...
>
> **Agent Kay:** There's always an Arquillian Battle Cruiser, or a Corillian Death Ray, or an intergalactic plague that is about to wipe out all life on this miserable little planet, and the only way these people can get on with their happy lives is that they DO NOT KNOW ABOUT IT!

It's up to heroes Kay and Jay to recognize and overcome the challenges of their Ordinary World.

> **Agent Kay:** We are the best kept secret in the galaxy. We monitor, license, and police all alien activity on the earth. We're your first, last, and only line of defense. We live in secret, we exist in shadow.
>
> **Agent Jay:** And we dress in black. (1)

The Ordinary World for healthcare consumers and providers is a world of contrasts: providers' views of what patients want from their financial experience often conflict directly with what patients say they want. It may appear that patients and providers operate on opposite sides of a cosmic divide. Patients face higher healthcare costs and deductibles, they receive healthcare bills they don't understand and want help paying their obligations but often end up confused and frustrated; not understanding what they need to do. Healthcare providers realize the need to engage with patients more frequently and more effectively, but they typically don't provide price estimates or combine prices for services on billing statements, offer flexible payment plans, or reach out to patients before care is given. As a result, patients unwittingly feed the villains that threaten providers: they are slow to pay balances due, become dissatisfied, and shift their loyalty to another institution, and providers face the downstream effects of increasing cost to collect and bad debt.

Let's take a closer look at each side of the healthcare payment divide.

Patients

Healthcare costs continue to rise for American families. For every dollar spent on healthcare in 2015, families paid 11 cents out of their own pockets and 28 cents after including insurance costs. In 2016, according to a JP Morgan Chase Institute analysis of out-of-pocket healthcare spending involving 2.3 million Chase customers between the ages of 18 and 64, families spent almost 2 percent of their take home pay on healthcare. (2)

Families are having trouble keeping up with healthcare costs, particularly the amounts they pay for deductibles. While health insurance premiums increased more (19 percent) than wages (11 percent) and inflation (6 percent), deductibles rose a staggering 63 percent in 2016. The number of families with high-deductible health plans increased by nearly 4 percent in 2017 alone. (3)

So how do patients deal with healthcare expenditures? First off, they prioritize. On the list of the most important bills to pay each month, mortgage and rent are tops, followed by utilities payments. Next come health insurance premiums. But actual medical bills are near the bottom. Seventy-two percent of consumers rank mortgage and rent as number one and 55 percent rank utilities as second, with 22 percent listing health insurance premiums as third. Paying medical bills comes in at 7 percent, just ahead of other bills and entertainment or discretionary spending, at 3 percent. (4) Actual medical bills are near the bottom.

As long as they are financially able, patients tend to pay their medical bills. But middle-class families can even be hard pressed to make payments. According to The Advisory Board, "patients aren't likely to pay medical bills greater than 5 percent of their household income." If the median U.S. income is $55,000, the threshold for payment then would be about $2,800, far less than a family's average deductible. (5)

Patients' satisfaction with their healthcare makes a huge difference. Patients who are fully satisfied with their care tend to pay in full 70 percent of the time or they pay a portion and intend to pay off the balance 95 percent of the time. Those who are dissatisfied pay in full only 22 percent of the time and intend to pay off the balance 50 percent of the time. (6)

Patients are worried and confused. More than half of consumers are concerned about being able to pay a medical bill less than one thousand dollars, 35 percent fret about paying a bill less than five hundred dollars, and 42 percent are perplexed about what they owe, according to a 2017 survey by HealthFirst Financial. (7)

Avadyne Health's own research bears out these observations. In the report, *Bridging the Gap: The Growing Disconnect Between Patient Expectations and the Healthcare Financial Experience*, Avadyne researchers noted the burden that rising healthcare costs place on American families:

- Forty-five percent of Americans polled by the Kaiser Family Foundation said they would have difficulty paying an unexpected medical bill of $500.
- The average deductible for even the least expensive Affordable Care Act Exchanges is $6,000 for an individual.
- Most people with private health insurance paid less than $500 in out-of-pocket expenses in 2015, but nearly 25 percent spent $1,000 or more, and 10 percent spent more than $2,000 in 2017.
- More than 66 percent of patients aren't paying their entire hospital bills, according to TransUnion Healthcare, largely because of more liability and higher deductible health insurance plans.
- On average, individual health insurance premiums and out-of-pocket expenditures will top $5,200 in 2018, according to Aon. (8)

For families who had difficulty paying their medical bills, Avadyne researchers found:

- Even with health insurance coverage, 25 percent of working age Americans had to change employment or their lifestyle to pay their medical bills, according to a Kaiser Family Foundation/New York Times survey.
- For 45 percent of individuals with insurance, medical bills had a major impact on their families. A little over 30 percent of these individuals had bills greater than $5,000 and 13 percent had bills of more than $10,000. (8)

What Do Patients Want?

Avadyne Health conducted a survey of five hundred healthcare consumers who received hospital care in the previous twelve months and incurred out-of-pocket expenses after insurance coverage. A third of these patients had expenses over five hundred dollars. The survey was conducted in early 2018 and primarily included individuals between the ages of fifty-three and seventy-one who were the major healthcare decision-makers for themselves or their families.

Among the patients in this survey, 84 percent pay nonhospital bills on time or early; 12 percent are sometimes late but not more than 30 days in arrears; 3 percent pay 30 or more days late; and 1 percent pay 60 or more days late. Far fewer pay hospital bills as quickly: only 29 percent make partial payment before treatment and the balance immediately after service; 13 percent make multiple payments; 53 percent delay payment until they receive information about their insurance benefits; and 5 percent wait as long as possible, often more than 60 days.

The survey was designed to investigate all aspects of the Patient Financial Experience—from initial conversations with hospital personnel about expected prices through backend interactions and the tools patients can use to make payments—and to determine how patients feel about the entire financial engagement. The survey showed that:

- One out of two patients say the continuity of their Patient Financial Experience was not satisfactory
- Two out of three say price estimates are needed, particularly Baby Boomers
- Two out of three believe an online payment portal would reduce or have no change on their overall satisfaction
- One out of two want a concierge to talk them through the financial experience

The factors most likely to improve satisfaction for patients with the financial experience were:

- Consolidation of costs for treatment in a single, easy-to-understand bill (56 percent of those surveyed)
- More engagement by hospital payment experts before arrival for treatment to help estimate costs (41 percent of survey respondents)
- A dedicated support person who would serve as a guide through the financial process (41 percent of respondents)

The factors that would not improve satisfaction were:

- Email or automated reminders about open balances (68 percent of survey respondents)
- Do-it-yourself payment portals (64 percent of respondents)
- More payment plans to extend payments over time (63 percent of those surveyed)

The Avadyne researchers concluded that patients want:

1. CONTINUITY. The disjointed and cumbersome financial experience that exists at most hospitals today is no longer acceptable to consumers. Most respondents (60 percent, across all age groups) expect continuity with the people, processes, billing, and payment tools from hospitals. Over half (55 percent) are less than satisfied with what has been offered so far. Siloed processes very quickly lead to a lack of trust and accounts that cannot be financially cleared prior to service.

Receiving individual statements from different providers for the same episode of clinical care is particularly confusing for consumers. Different ways of collecting payments and producing price estimates across touch points along the patient's healthcare journey engenders distrust.

Providers that use multiple vendors for patient collections further communicate inconsistency. Survey respondents report using an average of 4.1 different service providers (or 6.2 vendors for $1 billion + organizations) for patient collections. By working with fewer revenue cycle vendors, providers can create a more seamless financial experience for their patients from preservice to postservice.

2. HELP THROUGHOUT THE PAYMENT PROCESS. Over 50 percent of respondents say they want help and guidance from someone who understands their out-of-pocket expenses. Over 51 percent of patients feel that having a dedicated support person to walk them through the financial process would improve satisfaction. Millennials appear to expect more help, with 56 percent stating that this kind of assistance is very important to them. Younger patients have a greater interest in receiving reminders about balances. One out of every 2 patients wants financial guidance to come in the form of a concierge approach to their financial experience, from a helpful person via phone or online. Over half (56 percent) want be offered options proactively to help resolve out-of-pocket expenses, without having to seek the information out.

However, 55 percent of consumers report being less than satisfied when it comes to their hospital's ability to provide this type of financial help and guidance. When patients do receive guidance from a hospital resource, they give high ratings (66 percent satisfaction score) in terms of friendliness and professionalism. Interestingly, though, about one-third (35 percent) are less than satisfied when it comes to the clarity and helpfulness of these resources. Patients are often confused by terminology such as "deductible," and "coinsurance." Confusion quickly leads to mistrust—which results in bills that go unpaid or delayed. Revenue cycle leaders who embrace the role of educating patients about their coverage and the "why" behind their quoted liability amount are fostering the desired financial relationship with their patients.

3. SIMPLE, EASY-TO-UNDERSTAND BILLING STATEMENTS.

Patients are clear on this point: They want all their costs outlined in a single bill. Across all age groups, patients report that a single, consolidated billing statement is important to them.

Providers are struggling to meet these expectations, however. Thus, there is significant dissatisfaction among patients, particularly among the GenX group (60 percent) and Baby Boomers (50 percent). Millennials' dissatisfaction also remains high, at 43 percent.

Consumers not only want a single billing statement, but they also want providers to simplify the statement so it's clear what they owe, and consumers are quite dissatisfied with providers' inability to do this. This is particularly apparent in the over-70 age group (68 percent).

4. ESTIMATES OF WHAT THEY MUST PAY BEFORE THE SERVICE IS PERFORMED.

Preservice price estimates are important to 71 percent of respondents. In fact, consumers rank this as the most important factor impacting their healthcare financial experience.

But one out of three patients describes the process of receiving an estimate and explanation of out-of-pocket costs prior to service as less than satisfactory. Nearly half don't feel they are given enough information about their out-of-pocket expenses beforehand.

Many hospitals have begun offering preservice price estimates, or are in the process of doing so, in response to increased patient liability. It's not enough to give patients a dollar amount. Hospitals must provide good communication and enough information about estimates, because it's what patients want.

Patients reveal the most important issue in terms of their Financial Experience: Knowing the total cost of their care, including what insurance covers and what portion of the bill they are responsible for.

5. CONTROL. Consumers want a say in how their bills are delivered. Millennials speak the loudest (40 percent) in terms of ranking this feature and the impact it has on their Patient Financial Experience. It should come as no surprise that people accustomed to paying for purchases online on desktop PCs, mobile phones, or other devices should want the same from their hospital bills. Customers who pay power bills by texting a single letter quickly get used to the convenience it offers. Such payment options are not possible with healthcare bills, which may arrive weeks or months after the fact in the mailbox in hard-to-decipher paper statements. Respondents are not happy with their hospital's ability to customize the way bills are delivered based on the patient's preference (60 percent are less than satisfied). A one-size-fits-all approach simply does not work for the way today's patients financially interact with hospitals. Hospital statement delivery systems must accommodate generational preferences in the use of technology and patients' preferences in the way bills are delivered.

6. INFORMATION BEFORE THEY PAY THEIR BILLS. The vast majority (83 percent) of respondents pay their nonhospital bills on time or early. Yet more than half (58 percent) wait for insurance statements, or wait as long as they can, before paying their hospital bills. That percentage is higher (64 percent) among Baby Boomers, a group representing a growing portion of Medicare and Medicaid costs.

If providers build trustworthy financial relationships with their patients, patients' financial behavior will inevitably change, too. Those who habitually pay their other bills upfront need a good reason—in the form of a timely, accurate price estimate they can trust and rely on—to do the same with their hospital bills.

7. A FINANCIAL EXPERIENCE CONSISTENT WITH A POSITIVE RETAIL PURCHASE EXPERIENCE. Consumers across all age groups see no reason why their healthcare financial experience should not mirror the encounters they have with banking, credit cards, or other transactions. But healthcare providers are falling far short in an area that is increasingly important to consumers. Most respondents (57 percent) believe that their financial experience with healthcare expenses is not consistent with a good retail financial experience.

Can you imagine ordering a meal from a high-end restaurant that has no prices on its menu, provides separate bills for the appetizer, cocktails, and each course after the meal?

Confusion and mistrust would reign in this situation, as it does among patients today when something similar happens to them. Just as restaurant diners would surely go someplace else, so will healthcare consumers.

Amazon is, of course, a very successful company. But where did they start? They sold and resold books. So how did the company go from books to groceries and car parts? How did it become the place you go for virtually all your household items? The answer is customer service. They're meeting you where you want to be met from a technology and service standpoint and making it easy to do business with them.

It's important to provide excellent service clinically, but also make it easier for patients to do business with us in urgent care, the surgery center, the pediatric family practice, or the delivery unit. All patients should have the same great experience.

One of the things we're constantly thinking about on the revenue cycle side is how to meet patients in the medium that they want. Can they contact you on the phone, get text messages, or find what they need online? Do we provide the correct balance of self service and personally assisted mediums to meet the broad spectrum of patients and customers who interact with our health system? Can they easily schedule service, receive price estimates, apply for credit, request their patient records, or just easily pay their bills? We want to give patients flexibility and options, which historically they have not been able to receive. We want patients to expect and receive the highest level of customer service from us.

Bradley Tinnermon, Vice President Revenue Cycle and Revenue Integrity, Banner Health

Now, let's look at the other side of the cosmic divide.

HEALTHCARE PROVIDERS

Traditionally, hospitals and providers received almost all their reimbursement from insurers, and almost none from patients. That dynamic has shifted dramatically. Uncompensated care reached $38.3 billion in 2016, up from $35.7 billion in 2015, according to the American Hospital Association's Annual Survey of Hospitals. A significant portion of this can be attributed to unpaid patient bills. (9)

Initially, hospitals saw less bad debt from uninsured patients, due to twenty million additional insured Americans under the Affordable Care Act. An unintended consequence was the rise in high-deductible plans, causing patient payment portions to become more significant. This is a financial stressor, both for patients who bear the burden of the costs and for hospitals that absorb the lost revenue when bills go unpaid. (10)

Unpaid bills often stem from patients' poor satisfaction with the financial experience, and account for a portion of lost revenue for hospitals and healthcare systems. When patients choose another hospital, significant additional revenue is lost—estimated at over $1 million over a person's lifetime. It has become painfully apparent that more than just an unpaid co-pay or deductible is at stake. To compete in this environment, hospitals must adopt a new mind-set when it comes to patient liability resolution.

As patients take on more responsibility, hospitals face commensurate increases in bad debt. Already thin profit margins make it difficult—or impossible—for some hospitals to continue operations. Nationwide, about 80 rural hospitals have closed since 2010, according to the Chartis Center for Rural Health—and another 673 hospitals are in danger of shutting their doors. (11)

The situation couldn't be clearer. An April report from Moody's Investors Service shows that median operating cash flow for 160 not-for-profit and public hospitals declined to 8.1 percent in 2017, a level not seen since the 2008–09 recession. At the same time the American Hospital Association's 2018 Chartbook concluded that the percentage of hospitals with negative total and operating margins increased by the end of 2016 to 2008–09 levels. (12, 13)

Hospital leaders are turning to cost control as a result. The Advisory Board's Annual Health Care CEO Survey of 146 corporate hospital executives found that 62 percent are "extremely interested" in cost control and 56 percent are looking for "innovative approaches to expense reduction." The survey was conducted between December 2017 and March 2018. (14)

A 2017 survey of 150 hospital and health system executives found that 96 percent think "cost transformation" is at the top of their list of priorities. In addition to standard supply chain (68 percent), labor and productivity (66 percent), 60 percent of respondents intend to focus on revenue cycle enhancement. (15)

What Are Providers Missing?

The Bridging the Gap study conducted by Avadyne Health included surveys with representatives from 100 hospitals, with a fairly even split between hospitals that have net patient revenue of $300 million, $1 billion, and more than $1 billion. Nearly all (92 percent) respondents were classified as either executive manager or leaders of revenue cycle management within their institutions.

Avadyne's study reveals that healthcare providers know they must take a fresh look at the financial experience they are creating for patients. In fact, 28 percent name continuity in the Patient Financial Experience as the factor that will have the greatest impact on their organization's profit margins.

Survey respondents are concerned that patient financial responsibility and uncompensated care are growing and negatively impacting profit margins. They also recognize that driving preservice payments is integral to better positioning of the hospital financially.

Providers have worked hard to make it easier for patients to pay through easier-to-use and attractive online portals and a number of other payment options. Avadyne's research; however, reveals that patients expect more. The data shows that the entire financial experience needs to be analyzed, including the initial pre-service conversation, and every step along the way through final resolution or debt collection.

Revenue cycle leaders understand that the inability to financially clear accounts prior to service on the front end, and unpaid bills on the back end, are negatively impacting their margins (more so now than when insurers covered a larger portion of the total cost of care.)

Providers acknowledge the link between a good financial experience and the hospital's financial solvency, but actual practices tell a different story.

SOME KEY FINDINGS FROM THE SURVEY OF HEALTHCARE PROVIDERS:

1. ONLY ABOUT A THIRD (37 percent) OF PROVIDERS OFFER AN ESTIMATE OR EXPLANATION OF COSTS PRIOR TO SERVICE. In contrast, 65 percent of consumers say this is very important to them. In fact, getting an explanation of costs was ranked by 41 percent of patient respondents at the very top of the list of factors that would positively impact the financial experience. Yet only a minority of providers offers estimates, and price estimation is not a priority for other providers. This option ranked third on the list of actions providers intend to accomplish over the next several years.

Of the 55 percent of patients who do receive some type of estimate of costs prior to service, most are not fully satisfied, identifying lack of information as the main problem. Even providers rank themselves as only "OK" in this area (3.3 out of 5.0 in satisfaction). Perhaps most telling, revenue cycle leaders estimate that over one-quarter of Balance-After-Insurance estimates are inaccurate (such as having the wrong service, wrong benefits or wrong CPT code). These high inaccuracy rates are something CFOs and CEOs are largely unaware of, according to Avadyne's data, but something they would do well to prioritize. For both patients and hospitals, accuracy of estimates should be a priority.

2. MOST (55 percent) PROVIDERS DO NOT OFFER COMBINED BILLING STATEMENTS. Having a combined statement ranks high on the importance list for 50 percent of respondents. For the patient, multiple individual bills cause stress and confusion. Not uncommonly, patients receive bills even from physicians or entities they're unaware of. Surgical patients routinely receive separate bills from the surgeon,

the lab, the anesthesiologist, possibly a consulting doctor who reviewed their care, and more. It's easy to see how receiving a stack of bills without a cohesive explanation while recovering from surgery can cast a negative shadow over one's entire healthcare experience. Failure to address this top dissatisfier is a missed opportunity for positively impacting the Patient Financial Experience.

3. PROVIDERS KNOW THEIR BILLING STATEMENT AND PROCESSES NEED WORK. Almost half (47 percent) of providers are less than satisfied with their organization's current billing statement and processes. Only about a quarter (27 percent) offer flexible payment plans; just 9 percent offer the kind of pre-service outreach that patients want. Providers are aware they need to do more, but they are stymied by lack of clarity on how to fix the problem.

4. PROVIDERS ARE LARGELY FOCUSED ON BUILDING MECHANISMS TO HELP PATIENTS PAY. Avadyne's survey revealed that over 67 percent of providers feel they can improve the payment tools they employ. The data identified these top three priorities for providers: Emphasizing point-of-service payments (14 percent), offering payment portals (12 percent), and streamlining billing for services across the system (11 percent). While these are important goals, they aren't enough to move the needle on the patient's financial satisfaction meter.

Nearly 90 percent of organizations are offering phone support to patients, but very few (12 percent) are offering online support that is likely to be important to Millennials. Virtually all (93 percent) believe that a concierge service would improve their Patient Financial Experience. Payment portals are a piece of the puzzle, but a portal by itself won't meet the overarching need for hospitals to provide a cohesive, informative, and consistent experience that builds trust.

Earlier financial discussions, more accurate price estimates, and better communication throughout their financial experience are what's needed to gain patients' confidence and trust throughout their financial experience, and Revenue Cycle Champions know where to look for the information and other resources that will prove the case to hospital leadership.

> **Agent Kay:** [Standing in front of a newsstand]: We'll check the hot sheets.
>
> **Agent Jay:** *These* are the hot sheets?
>
> **Agent Kay:** Best investigative reporting on the planet. Read The New York Times if you want, they get lucky sometimes.
>
> **Agent Jay:** I cannot believe you're looking for tips in the supermarket tabloids.
>
> **Agent Kay:** [Pointing to a front page article about farmer's stolen skin] Not looking for. Found.

Questions & Considerations

- For the same episode of care, do patients receive multiple statements that could be consolidated?

- Do you provide price estimates prior to service?

- How many vendors do you use in the Patient Financial Experience?

- Do you have a concierge service approach?

- Do you use terminology that confuses patients?

- Do you have an easy-to-understand patient billing statement?

- Do you provide statements electronically and by other electronic means (text)?

- Do you offer multiple electronic/online payment options?

CHAPTER 3

The Call to Action

A dystopian future is perceived as a simulated reality known as the Matrix, created by sentient machines to subdue the human population and use heat and electrical activity from the human body as an energy source. Cybercriminal and computer programmer Neo suspects this truth and is being drawn by rebel leader Trinity into a rebellion against the machines.

Trinity: Right now all I can tell you is that you're in danger. I brought you here to warn you.

Neo: Of what?

Trinity: They're watching you, Neo.

Neo: Who is?

Trinity: Please just listen. I know why you're here, Neo. I know what you've been doing. I know why you hardly sleep, why you live alone, and why night after night you sit at your computer. You're looking for him. I know, because I was once looking for the same thing. And when he found me, he told me I wasn't really looking for him. I was looking for an answer. It's the question that drives us mad. It's the question that brought you here. You know the question just as I did.

Neo: What is the Matrix?

Trinity: The answer is out there, Neo. It's looking for you. And it will find you, if you want it to. —The Matrix, Warner Brothers, 1999. (1)

The Call to Action in fiction comes in many forms, as Christopher Vogler observes in The Writer's Journey—a message or messenger, an event, an ah-ha awakening or moment of realization, or simple frustration with the status quo and a recognition of ways to counteract it. "The Call…is a process of selection. An unstable situation arises in a society and someone volunteers or is chosen to take responsibility," Vogler writes. (2)

An unstable situation is present in the U.S. healthcare system. Hospitals are facing significant challenges on many fronts—legislative, financial, regulatory, and operational—that are out of their direct control. However, when it comes to improving the Patient Financial Experience, there is plenty of opportunity for hospitals and health systems to more closely align patient expectations and reality. Providers are working hard to create a positive clinical experience under the new value-based care reimbursement models. Now they must work to create a positive financial experience for patients—by taking a holistic approach. The research gathered in Avadyne's Bridging the Gap report provides a clear roadmap for providers to replace the current way of doing things with a New World that more directly meets patients' expectations.

Here are some actions revenue cycle champions can take to answer The Call and improve the Patient Financial Experience:

LEARN HOW TO MEASURE AND MONITOR SATISFACTION WITH THE PATIENT FINANCIAL EXPERIENCE

Surveys are the primary way organizations are measuring the Patient Financial Experience, according to Avadyne study data. Unfortunately, only about 5 percent of patients typically respond to surveys. What's more, very few surveyors have real-time access to patient communications and analytics. Many rely on the number of complaints that reach senior leadership about billing and payment issues to gauge satisfaction, and over 20 percent aren't doing anything at all to measure Patient Financial Experience. (3)

The patient experience remains a top priority at all healthcare organizations, but measurement typically focuses on the clinical side. Quality clinical care is critical to the health and safety of patients, and hospitals use it to differentiate themselves within a marketplace. However, the financial experience is equally important to overall patient satisfaction. It can set hospitals apart from competitors as surely as world-class clinical care. Conversely, the financial experience can negatively impact patients' overall opinion of the institution, even if clinical care is excellent.

To cite an example, over 90 percent of patients reported satisfaction with their primary care physician, in a survey commissioned by the Physicians Foundation. At the same time, many patients voiced concerns regarding healthcare costs and medical debt. This brings home the point that, even if patients are satisfied with the clinical care received, a negative financial experience can cloud their overall perception of their care. (4)

What an individual patient perceives can quickly spread in messages to others, especially if the patient chooses to publicly voice dissatisfaction. Over a third (39 percent) of dissatisfied patients don't recommend their hospital to a friend or family member, and 30 percent do not return to the hospital for service in the future. As noted in the previous chapter, dissatisfied patients are less likely to pay their bills; so a poor financial experience can become a source of lost revenue for a hospital. (5)

There are many well-established metrics used to measure the quality of clinical care, but financial experience is difficult to score. Many providers use predictive analytics, typically in the form of propensity-to-pay tools, to determine a patient's ability to pay. However; providers must also factor in the patient's willingness to pay by identifying factors that influence patient satisfaction with the financial experience.

Hospitals also must be able to track recurring issues that tend to cause dissatisfaction and intervene before a problem escalates, reaches "a point of no return" for an unhappy patient, results in an uncollected balance, and an increase in bad debt despite remedial efforts to salvage the situation. Technology to measure every word of every call is needed, so that trends driving dissatisfaction can be identified and resolution can occur in realtime.

ENGAGE WITH PATIENTS EARLIER AND MORE OFTEN THROUGHOUT THEIR HEALTHCARE FINANCIAL JOURNEY

Pushing financial conversations to the front end of the process with early, accurate price estimates allows providers to engage with patients before they even come in the door. By doing so, providers can position themselves from the beginning as a trusted advisor who is concerned about their patients' well-being in a holistic manner, from both clinical and financial perspectives. Even if a provider is not able to provide pre-service price estimates, the revenue cycle can engage in the account resolution process earlier to positively affect patient satisfaction.

Prediction technology helps providers identify patients who may have difficulty meeting their financial obligation so a provider can intervene ahead of time to offer payment options and plans that align with the individual patient's needs, demonstrate the institution's willingness to work with the patient, and build trust. Waiting to address the financial discussion until after service has been given diminishes the patient's trust in the hospital—and does long-term damage to the overall relationship between the patient and the hospital.

DEVELOP A SCORING MECHANISM

Uncompensated care costs continue to eat away at providers' razor-thin bottom line, but revenue cycle leaders struggle to make the connection between uncompensated care and patient satisfaction. It should be clear, a negative Patient Financial Experience increases the likelihood that care will be uncompensated. Despite the imperative to reduce uncompensated care, the Patient Financial Experience, and how to fix it, remains largely a mystery for healthcare providers. Less than 3 percent of hospital respondents in Avadyne's survey utilize any type of scoring that specifically targets the Patient Financial Experience. For years hospitals have leveraged various methodologies to gauge satisfaction, such as Hospital Consumer Assessment of Healthcare Providers and Systems (HCAHPS). However, these tools have very little bearing on patient satisfaction with the financial experience. Information gathered by these tools is not specific to financial interactions, nor is it offered in a timely fashion so revenue cycle executives can react quickly.

Providers should consider a targeted scoring system that measures total patient financial satisfaction across every engagement and every touch point. This would allow providers to learn exactly what's driving patient satisfaction—or lack thereof. Both speech transcription analytics and acoustic measurements across calls, chats, surveys, text messages, emails, and Twitter are needed to assess key metrics involving call emotion, patient escalation, call profanity, call effort, wait times, abandonment rates, and number of single-call resolutions. This type of proactive scoring gives providers enough data to take action in real time and improve patient financial satisfaction and revenue.

OFFER A CONCIERGE SERVICE

It's no longer good enough to have people in your billing department react to inbound patient inquiries. Online chat and phone support must be built into all billing access points to offer assistance whenever and wherever it's needed. Support for patients identified at significant risk for escalation must be proactive and expeditiously identify the right financial approach for each patient.

GET ON THE SAME PAGE

Hospital executives and the revenue cycle leadership often disagree about just how well they are doing with the Patient Financial Experience. Some key findings from the Avadyne survey:

- When asked how satisfied they were with the type and breadth of patient payment offerings, executives are less satisfied (43 percent) than revenue cycle leaders (64 percent).
- CFOs are more inclined to prioritize point-of-service collections and payment portals, whereas revenue cycle leaders more heavily weight the overall continuity of the Patient Financial Experience, the adequacy of preservice conversations, and the accuracy of price estimations.
- CEOs believe that the lack of automation and innovative technology have the most bearing on the organization's

bottom line when it comes to patient liability resolution. Revenue cycle leaders report that a preservice collections capability exerts the greatest impact.

- Making the financial process a seamless, positive engagement at every contact point is more of a priority for revenue cycle leaders than it is for CEOs.

A PERSONALIZED APPROACH

Larry Van Horn, executive director of health affairs at Vanderbilt University's Owen Graduate School of Management, explained in a March, 2016, report for the *Tennessean*, why more than half of hospital bills are not paid: "There needs to be a collective mind-set shift. Hospitals have to be more transparent in billing and pricing, while patients have to be prepared to set money aside to pay for their healthcare. People are going to need to plan for healthcare just like they do for all kinds of services they already pay for out-of-pocket." (6)

Relying on traditional bad debt write-offs in the face of increasing patient liability spells financial disaster for hospitals. Healthcare providers need a revenue cycle strategy that promotes a positive financial experience for all patients. Delivering the financial experience that patients want ensures that liabilities will be resolved in the near-term and that patients will remain loyal for years to come. No two patient experiences or expectations are exactly alike, so revenue cycle processes should take into account not only individual but also generational preferences and tailor actions accordingly.

These are the elements of The Call to Action for revenue cycle champions. Are you ready to answer this Call?

> Morpheus, leader of the rebels against the Matrix, gives Neo a choice: accept or refuse the Call to Action.

Morpheus: I'm trying to free your mind, Neo. But I can only show you the door. You're the one that has to walk through it.

Questions & Considerations

- How do you measure the Patient Financial Experience?

- Do you engage patients in preservice conversations?

- Do you score the Patient Financial Experience?

- Do you use speech analytics or acoustic measurements?

- Do you offer a concierge-type level of service?

- Is there continuity in the Patient Financial Experience?

- Are payment options available across the revenue cycle?

CHAPTER 4

Resistance and Threshold

Prince N'Jobu is the younger brother of T'Chaka, the King of Wakanda, and an agent of the War Dogs secret police. He betrayed his own people, and in the process aided black market arms profiteer Ulysses Klaue, by getting the precious metal vibranium out of Wakanda. His intention was to allow oppressed people all over the world to possess the power of the material. N'Jobu was confronted by T'Chaka and later killed by his brother. His death led his son, Erik Stevens, to go on a long journey of vengeance to avenge his father's death and challenge the King of Wakanda for leadership.

> **N'Jobu:** I observed for as long as I could. Their leaders have been assassinated. Communities flooded with drugs and weapons. They are overly policed and incarcerated. All over the planet, our people suffer because they don't have the tools to fight back. With vibranium weapons they can overthrow all countries, and Wakanda can rule them all, the right way!
> *The Black Panther*, Screen Gems, 2018 (1)

Even after accepting their Calls to Action, heroes hesitate, delay, or avoid taking the first steps because of existing forces of Resistance or the major problems that stand in their way. For those on the Revenue Cycle Hero's Journey, the difficulties are long-standing ones, and they are not easy to overcome.

At a closed-door meeting including members of the C-Suite, the topic turns to the Patient Experience. No surprise there—it's been a top priority for Wakanda General Hospital for years.

The revenue cycle leader leans back and sips her coffee, eagerly awaiting the chance to present the latest scores from Press Ganey that pertain to registration. So when the discussion moves from clinical departments to other hospital areas, the revenue cycle leader concisely summarizes the improved satisfaction numbers.

Suddenly, the CFO interjects, "What we really need are specifics on the Patient Financial Experience. What can you tell us about that?"

The revenue cycle director, momentarily flummoxed, begins to rattle off the latest HCAHPS scores (there is, of course, some significant improvement to brag about!).

"Yes," says the CEO, "but those are largely clinical measures. We're interested in the financial side of satisfaction. And anyway—aren't survey completion rates pretty low?"

The revenue cycle director shifts to postcall surveys of discharged patients, which show a pretty impressive uptick in satisfaction rates. Unfortunately, someone in the group quickly points out that these, too, have dismal completion rates. (Read: These measurements don't really count for much!)

The revenue cycle director finally takes a "warm and fuzzy" tactic, recounting a heartfelt letter from a patient who couldn't rave enough about the financial counseling she received during her hospital stay. (Later, when the CFO asks for specifics to learn why the patient was so happy, he finds out that the charges had been written off because the original price estimate was wildly inaccurate—an example of a financial experience no hospital can afford to deliver!)

The Problem with Patient Satisfaction Scores

Hospitals do, of course, closely track their patient satisfaction scores. But what do those general, organization-wide scores really tell the hospital about financial experiences? Frankly, next to nothing. The data is far too vague, showing only where a department finishes—in the 10th, 50th, or even 98th percentile—for responses to the question: "How satisfied were you with your registration process?"

One issue is that the general public has little to no understanding of the revenue cycle and its various functions in the hospital. Most have no idea about the difference between preregistration, registration, and scheduling, or between patient access and the business office. Patients asked to rate their registration experience may think of the day they called to schedule the procedure, when they preregistered, when they arrived on the day of the procedure, when they were asked for a balance, or something else entirely. The hospital really has no way of knowing, unless the person happens to write in a comment to explain the reason for a high or low score.

The question then becomes: What does a revenue cycle leader do with this incomplete information? If satisfaction scores for their department or area go from the 70th percentile to the 90th percentile, that leader will certainly be eager to share the improvement at the next board meeting. However, a big piece of the satisfaction puzzle is missing—namely, how it relates to the financial experience in its entirety. What does the increase—or decrease—in satisfaction scores mean? What did people like and what did they dislike about their financial experience? What held them back from giving a perfect score?

Points of Resistance

The patient is an important part of the paying equation, and an unhappy patient/payer simply may not return to the hospital—even if things run perfectly on the clinical side. However, there is no standard, well-established way to capture patient satisfaction with the revenue cycle operation.

The HCAHPS survey, the first national, standardized survey that ties performance results to hospital reimbursements, evaluates key areas of the patient experience. HCAHPS, also known as the CAHPS Hospital Survey, is a survey instrument and data collection methodology for measuring and publicly reporting patients' perceptions of their hospital experience. The HCAHPS survey is administered to a random sample of adult patients across medical conditions between forty-eight hours and six weeks after discharge by mail, telephone, mail with telephone follow-up, or through an interactive voice recognition system (IVR). (2)

Three broad goals have shaped HCAHPS. First, the survey is designed to produce data about patients' perspectives of care that allow objective and meaningful comparisons of hospitals on topics that are important to consumers. Second, public reporting of the survey results creates new incentives for hospitals to improve quality of care. Third, public reporting serves to enhance accountability in healthcare by increasing transparency of the quality of hospital care provided in return for the public investment. With these goals in mind, the Centers for Medicare & Medicaid Services (CMS) and the HCAHPS Project Team have taken substantial steps to ensure the survey is credible, useful, and practical. (2)

While many hospitals collect information on patient satisfaction for their own internal use, HCAHPS allows comparisons across hospitals locally, regionally, and nationally. The HCAHPS survey asks discharged patients twenty-seven questions about their recent hospital stay. Eighteen of these questions cover critical aspects of hospital care (communication with nurses and doctors, the responsiveness of hospital staff), the hospital environment (cleanliness and quietness), and focused communications (about pain management, medicines, and discharge). Only two questions fall outside the clinical sphere: an overall rating for hospital and the willingness to give the hospital a good word: Rate the hospital on a scale of 0 to 10. Yes or no: would you recommend the hospital to others? (2)

In addition to the fact that none of the HCAHPS questions directly measures financial management, the survey collects information on only a small cohort of patients—completion rates are 30 percent nationwide. And patients who complete the surveys tend to fall at the extremes—the "best" and the "worst" ends of the spectrum.

Postcall surveys are even worse: only 6 percent of patients respond, and they, too, tend to be at the polar ends of the feedback loop. Phone surveys asking patients about their financial encounters seem to be right on target. After all, they're focused solely on the financial encounter. With such low response rates, however, the surveys end up ignoring the vast majority of patients. As for the patients who actually do complete the phone surveys, the population is skewed. Avadyne analysts have found it's usually either very happy or very unhappy people who are willing to talk about the best or the worst experience ever. With a survey population of mostly outliers, interpreting the data becomes a pointless exercise. With mostly outliers forming the survey sample, interpretation of the data is treacherous or a pointless exercise. Even if survey findings point in a distinctly upward or downward trend, what does that really mean for overall satisfaction for patients across the board? Are most patients satisfied, disgruntled, or exasperated? No one really knows. (3)

Manual audits of random calls are well-intentioned, but woefully inadequate. Revenue cycle employees are worth their weight in gold when it comes to helping patients navigate their liability, but they cannot assess financial satisfaction in a comprehensive way on their own or accurately or comprehensively use the information to identify trends, fuel continuous improvement efforts, and protect short- and long-term revenue.

With no generally recognized, solid tools for measurement, healthcare organizations are left to their own devices to define and calculate the Patient Financial Experience. A 2016 survey by HBI found that, while most organizations do try to monitor patient satisfaction with financial management, metrics vary from hospital to hospital. The analytic tools have not been developed specifically for capturing patients' satisfaction with the financial side. Instead, they adapt existing measures to help shed insights on the matter, including statistics on upfront collection rates or point-of-service collection success, the number of days of revenue in credit balances, call abandonment rates, and registration wait times, but they don't take the next step and link the measures with satisfaction. (4)

Some hospitals fail to measure the full Patient Financial Experience at all. They gather information about their call wait times, call abandonment rates, and the percentage of accounts that are sent to bad debt, but how these metrics relate to patient satisfaction remains a mystery.

Others resort to tracking the number of complaints about the revenue cycle department or characterize complaints by their type. Revenue cycle leaders may learn something by taking this type of approach. For instance, they may notice an uptick in complaints regarding a particular registrar or a risk in complaints from patients with a particular insurance plan that just tightened its timeframes for authorizations. But complaint-based insights carry the risk that it's just the loudest, unhappiest voices that are being heard, and all other interactions are being ignored.

Where do these forces of Resistance leave the revenue cycle leader? Revenue cycle leaders have few choices: measure patient satisfaction on the basis of net patient revenue—or go by gut instinct: Is the Patient Financial Experience getting somewhat better, staying the same, or plummeting badly? They just don't know, because they don't have valid and reliable scoring methods. At the next board meeting when the topic of the Patient Financial Experience comes up, if a leader can point to is HCAHPS surveys or postcall surveys, she's coming up empty-handed, and everyone else know it.

The Threshold

What the revenue cycle needs are specifics concerning each aspect of the financial engagement process and how it influences the overall Patient Financial Experience by itself and in total: how the percentage of preservice financial clearance calls relate to overall patient satisfaction numbers, how additional training in collections is affecting bad debt, how co-pay collection, price estimation, financial counseling, charity care screening, payment plans, patient payment portals—and everything in between—operate together in a seamless fashion. But existing measurement tools—or their absence—just get in the way.

What's Needed?

To accurately and confidently score the Patient Financial Experience, the revenue cycle director needs to measure satisfaction for 100 percent of the touch points across the entire revenue cycle. This will allow:

- The revenue cycle leader to rely on the data to tell an accurate story.
- Other hospital leaders to trust that the data is creating a true picture of whether employees provide a world-class financial experience or a subpar one.

- Data analysts to pinpoint the reasons why scores dip: Are employees using the correct call opening? Are they confirming the balance, showing empathy, and providing education?
- The CFO to answer questions on the finer points of financial encounters that will benefit from further investment, including specialized training or new processes like a preservice financial discussion program, a more informative price estimate process, or more customer-friendly billing statements.
- The revenue cycle leader to hone in on specific areas and learn: Is the newly implemented co-pay collection initiative in labor and delivery negatively impacting satisfaction? Was the recent investment in specialized training justified; did it achieve the increases in overall satisfaction across the revenue cycle we anticipated? Did a change in the scheduling process that has decreased "no authorization" claims denials also increase satisfaction among those patients?

A full-scale, technology-based scoring system can also give the revenue cycle leader a chance to turn negative trends around, before it's too late to recapture lost market share. Let's take the example of dissatisfaction that's stemming from claims denials due to "no authorization." If the Patient Financial Experience score dips suddenly, and it's linked to a recent change in payer requirements, action can be taken to prevent further denials. New scheduling processes can be put into place to accommodate authorization timeframes of up to seven business days, for instance, to eliminate both denied claims as well as the dissatisfaction that comes from having to reschedule a procedure.

The moment the topic turns to the Patient Experience at the next meeting of the C-Suite, the revenue cycle leader can perk up and deliver this killer opening: "We identified three problems with the Patient Financial Experience in the last quarter. We implemented changes to fix each one, and in this quarter our score increased from a C to an A-minus.

"By targeting the problem spots that triggered dissatisfied patients, we feel comfortable setting a very ambitious goal for the next quarter. I'm thrilled to say we're on track to meet that goal," she continues.

Shining with pride, the revenue cycle leader can explain that fewer accounts are being placed in bad debt, timing in the placement of and first payment on accounts is improving, and new patient access training and processes are in the works. Each of these changes is driving a positive Patient Financial Experience and helping to place the hospital in a stronger financial position than the competition.

Next, the director can proudly share a story about a pregnant patient who found out she was underinsured and had a whopping five-thousand dollar deductible. The woman was offered an early pay discount and no-interest payment plan allowing her to have her baby in the hospital and leave with a healthy infant and less financial worry. An example of not only a positive experience but also revenue to the hospital.

In another patient encounter—this one, about a cancer patient who faced complex and expensive treatment but was uninsured. The patient qualified for Medicaid after hospital financial counselors helped her to apply, received initial therapy, and was already scheduled for a follow-up surgery. An example not only of revenue to the hospital but also the opportunity to ensure follow-up medical care, improving the patient's continuity of care and potentially saving her life.

These stories are not simple anecdotes; there are numbers to back them all up. And, based on the numbers, maybe for the first time, everyone in the leadership team sees value: It's no accident that feel-good stories like these coincide with decreased bad debt, increased upfront collections, and shorter A/R, and the C-Suite is paying attention. The revenue cycle director can talk about the status of Balance After Insurance (BAI) accounts, the volume of accounts routing to bad debt, and many other accounts receivable metrics—all leading to an individual and holistic score for the measurement of patient financial satisfaction and experience.

The revenue cycle director can demonstrate how the numbers are moving in the right direction—and the plans for the ones that aren't. No need to wait for angry complaints to come rolling in. If the score goes down, the revenue cycle team can act immediately—just as the clinical team would do if a patient's blood pressure plummeted. Just as a changing vital sign wouldn't be ignored, a change in a critical financial score would be addressed immediately. A low score on the Patient Financial Experience meter isn't a cause for alarm, it's cause for change—maybe more training is needed to collect co-pays in the ED during the night shift—or preservice financial clearance calls are being made only 80 percent of the time when they should be done at least 90 percent of the time.

Perhaps the patient access department needs training, staffing, and technology resources? Now the revenue cycle director can justify the investments, because they can be linked to the Patient Financial Experience. Maybe a couple of board members hadn't thought specifically about the Patient Financial Experience, but they're certainly thinking about it now. The CFO had thought long and hard about it, but didn't really grasp it as being something separate and distinct from the overall patient experience. The CEO was unaware of the full extent of the long-term impact of an individual's Patient Financial Experience.

With Patient Financial Experience watched as closely as thirty-day readmissions for heart failure, the organization is poised for success. Patients—yes, even those who owe much more money than they ever expected—can leave fully satisfied with the care they received—both clinically and financially. The hospital can be assured of financial solvency, while competitors may struggle to push back against declining revenue that is somehow linked—but exactly how, competitors can't say—to poor satisfaction.

Adding numbers to patients' financial satisfaction is a definite game-changer:

- Numbers give the revenue cycle the kind of clout it has been looking for—almost overnight—because there's a clear way to justify investments everyone suspected were needed but no one could point to direct bottom-line benefit.
- Data gives the revenue cycle leader a seat at the table when decisions are being made about how and why to invest in resources or technology.
- Data is the bedrock foundation upon which all such investment and quality improvement decisions are made. Otherwise, how would hospitals know whether a costly new tool was a smart outlay or a total waste of resources?
- Even relatively minor purchasing decisions are almost always supported with ample amounts of data. If the return on investment can't be supported with numbers, you can bet a minor—or a major purchasing decision—won't be made.
- Hospital leaders want data to support claims that investment in a better price-estimate tool would improve patient satisfaction. The "hook" of improving the Patient

Experience may get attention, but numbers have to back it up.

Let's keep in mind that The Patient Experience hasn't always been a top priority for hospitals. For many decades hospitals didn't even measure satisfaction or consider it except as an afterthought. So why is the Patient Experience commanding so much attention at this particular point in time? Patient-centered models of care are one reason. Another is that higher patient experience scores are linked to higher hospital profitability. Hospitals with "excellent" patient ratings between 2008 and 2014 had a net margin of 4.7 percent, on average, as compared to just 1.8 percent for hospitals with "low" ratings. (6)

The Threshold has been crossed.

The Black Panther's real name is T'Challa, king and protector of the fictional African nation of Wakanda. Along with possessing enhanced abilities achieved through ancient Wakandan rituals of drinking the essence of the heart-shaped herb, T'Challa also relies on his proficiency in science, rigorous physical training, hand-to-hand combat skills, and access to wealth and advanced Wakandan technology to combat his enemies.

> **T'Challa:** Wakanda will no longer watch from the shadows. We cannot. We must not. We will work to be an example of how we, as brothers and sisters on this earth, should treat each other. Now, more than ever, the illusions of division threaten our very existence. We all know the truth: more connects us than separates us. But in times of crisis the wise build bridges, while the foolish build barriers. We must find a way to look after one another, as if we were one single tribe. (1)

Questions & Considerations

- How do you measure the Patient Financial Experience?

- Are all encounters included or limited in your measurement of the Patient Financial Experience?

- Do you have a scorecard across the revenue cycle for all Key Performance Indicators (KPIs)?

CHAPTER 5

The Journey

A teenager wakes up inside an underground elevator known as the Box with no memory of his identity. A group of boys greet him in a large grassy area called the Glade. The Glade is enclosed by tall stone walls that form a Maze behind a pair of closed gates. After spending years in the Glade, the boys (Gladers) have formed a rudimentary society, each with his own specialized tasks. Their leader, Alby, tells the boy, Thomas, that the Maze is the only way out.

Thomas: "We're trapped here, aren't we?"

Newt: For the moment, but…you see those guys, there…by the fire? Those are the Runners. And that guy in the middle there, that's Minho. He's the Keeper of the Runners. Now, every morning, when those doors open, they run the maze, mapping it, memorizing it, trying to find a way out.

Thomas: How long have they been looking?

Newt: Three years.

Thomas: And they haven't found anything?

Newt: It's a lot easier said than done. Listen…[metallic grinding noises.] Hear that? It's the Maze, changing. It changes every night.

Thomas: How is that even possible?

Newt: You can ask the people who put us in here, if you ever meet the bastards. Listen, the truth is…the Runners are the only ones who really know what's out there. They are the strongest and the fastest of us all. And it's a good thing, too…because if they don't make it back here before those doors close…then they are stuck out there for the night, and no one has ever survived a night in the Maze.
The Maze Runner, 20th Century Fox, 2014 (1)

This phase of Joseph Campbell's Hero's Journey narrative tests the hero, putting him or her through a series of trials and tribulations that prepare for the Transformation and the New World ahead.

This is a time when the hero finds allies who can provide special services or information and often become long-lasting friends. This testing stage also gives the opportunity for the hero to create a team who will help make plans, rehearse ways of approaching hurdles, and overcome obstacles along the way.

Thomas: But why would Alby go into the Maze? I mean, he's not a Runner.

Newt: [while chopping a tree by its roots] Things are different now. Alby went to retrace Ben's footsteps before sundown. Are you gonna help?

Thomas: Okay, so he's gonna go back to where Ben was just stung, and…

Newt: Alby knows what he's doing, all right? He knows better than any of us.

Thomas: What does that mean?

Newt: Well, it's like you've heard, yeah? Every month, the Box sends up a new arrival—but someone had to be first, right? Someone had to have spent a whole month in the Glade, alone. That was Alby. I mean, it can't have been easy; but, when those other boys started coming up, one after the other, he saw the truth, and he learned that the most important thing is that we all have each other, because we're all in this together. (1)

And then there are the enemies or villains who place conflict directly in the hero's path.

Ava Paige: Well…I think it's safe to say the Maze Trials were a complete success. I wasn't expecting so many survivors, but… the more the merrier. Thomas continues to surprise and impress; and, for now, they seem to have taken the bait. It's too soon to say, but…they could be the key to everything. So let's move forward. It's time now to begin…Phase Two. (1)

The Journey from the revenue cycle of today to the New World of tomorrow can easily be sidetracked by trials and challenges that have preyed upon healthcare providers for years or recently intensified. I have brought them to life here as villains you are all, unfortunately, far too familiar with:

- Slow Pay and Bad Debt
- Patient Complaints and Dissatisfaction

- Ineffective Training
- Cost to Collect

Let's take a look at each one and see how revenue cycle leaders of today can vanquish their villains. Because the Journey has many steps, we'll look at two of these villains—Slow Pay/Bad Debt and Complaints and Dissatisfaction—in this chapter and Ineffective Training and Cost to Collect in the next chapter.

Slow Pay

Patient payments are a major concern for healthcare CFOs and revenue cycle leaders. Research from various sources, including the Healthcare Financial Management Association and the Medical Group Management Association, indicates that the percentage of revenue collected from patients has jumped from 10 percent in 2002 to 30 percent in 2016. (2)

It's not just the proportion of revenue that now comes directly from patients, it is also because of the difficulties associated with collecting on patient accounts. Nearly half of all patient financial responsibility goes uncollected—one study found that two-thirds of patients are not paying off their hospital bills—and the likelihood of a patient paying a bill of more than five-thousand dollars is only about 40 percent. (3)

Patients also take longer to pay healthcare bills. According to Becker's Hospital CFO Report, 70 percent of providers recently reported that it takes a month or longer, on average, to collect payment from a patient. The Kaiser Family Foundation reported that 20 percent of insured patients had a hard time paying off their medical expenses in 2016. What's more, healthcare payments are lower priorities for patients, ranking seventh after the mortgage, car and cell phone payments, and credit card bills. Of course, the longer it takes for a patient to pay, the less likely—and more costly—it is to actually collect. (4, 5, 6)

The Revenue Improver

Enter the Revenue Improver. This revenue cycle hero can collect payments sooner, reduce the number of collection calls made to patients, improve the accuracy and cut the cost of producing billing statements, and give patients 24/7 online access to payment information. How? By interacting with patients sooner, taking the mystery out of price estimates, and offering a patient-friendly payment portal.

EARLY ACCESS

Patients are more likely to pay if they understand what they're responsible for and have someone they trust to talk to. In our experience 26 percent of patients arrange for payment upfront when their providers engage them in financial discussions early in the healthcare process. For example, a large healthcare system saw a 65 percent increase in recoveries and a 24 percent decrease in bad debt write-offs. (7)

Nevertheless, providers' discussions with patients about their payment responsibilities and options tend to follow the traditional pattern: they occur after services have been delivered or not at all. Think of the timing: A patient receives a surprise medical bill or an unexpected call about payment of an existing bill. What's the reaction? Dissatisfaction, certainly, but worse—feelings of confusion and anxiety. There should be no surprises when it comes to a healthcare bill, and contact with providers about financial concerns should be expected—even desired—to get information and assistance. If providers wait too long to start their conversations with patients, they quickly run out of options.

Conversations with patients need to happen before services are delivered not only to identify and explain to the patient which scheduled services will or will not be covered by their insurance plan, but also to request that patients cover their out-of-pocket costs at the point of service. A well-planned and staffed Early Patient Access operation can then result in:

- Achieving 80 percent of the point-of-service collection potential
- Counseling 100 percent of patients with outstanding balances
- Explaining charity-care guidelines to patients who may qualify (8)

The underlying point: conversations need to occur at a time when patients can make choices, when:

- Revenue cycle employees with healthcare and insurance know-how can handle a financial situation that, at first glance, may seem unresolvable.
- Financial counselors can screen for Medicaid eligibility and charity care, obtain authorizations for services, offer payment plans, obtain an exception from the payer if the hospital is out of its network so the patient can continue receiving services, reschedule, or get a referral for service at an in-network facility.
- Patients can simply choose another healthcare provider.

PRICE ESTIMATES

Earlier in this book you'll remember that we discussed the Avadyne Bridging the Gap survey. A particularly interesting finding was that two out of three patients felt they needed preservice price estimates. Patients also rated access to out-of-pocket cost estimates as the second most important factor affecting their satisfaction with a healthcare provider. Providers, on the other hand, rated price estimates as second to last. (9)

But price estimates can be tricky, and frankly, providing no estimates at all is better than giving patients incomplete or inaccurate ones. Consider these examples:

A patient naturally chooses to have surgery at Hospital B, instead of Hospital A, when the price quote is six hundred dollars less. But Hospital B miscalculates the cost. It does not use the proper diagnosis codes, fails to factor in an additional service, and does not closely verify recent changes in the patient's insurance coverage. The result: a surprise bill that wipes out all the expected savings and adds more to the amount due.

A patient who needs to get a tonsillectomy for her son is price-shopping. She hasn't gotten insurance coverage through one of the health insurance exchanges; so the cost of the surgery will have to be paid entirely out-of-pocket. After contacting a few hospitals in the area, the patient selects the one with the lowest quote for the surgery. Two months later she receives a bill that's one thousand dollars more than the estimate. When she questions the amount, she's told that the estimate was just that—an estimate. She does not know that the price discrepancy was due to an additional procedure done at the time of surgery, nor does she realize she could have been placed on a low-interest payment plan.

A woman is scheduled for gastric bypass surgery and assumes her health plan covers it, since a colleague had the same surgery the year before and the insurer paid the bill. Unbeknown to the patient, the health plan now excludes this type of surgery from its coverage plan, and she is responsible for the full cost of the procedure.

The price estimates in these examples, and others too numerous to mention, are inaccurate, incomplete, inconsistent, and misleading. Often they're not only poorly done; they're also poorly communicated. What patients need, instead, are robust estimates that take into account the complexities of healthcare services and the patient's insurance coverage. Technology is essential here. Price estimates should be generated in real time and incorporate APCs, DRGs, and CPT codes, break down payer contracts by specific services, and use claims data that automatically updates your system every time a claim is paid.

Revenue cycle employees also need to know how to utilize estimation tools to ensure the proper diagnosis codes are applied and the insurance information is appropriate for this patient at this time. They need to be trained to speak with confidence not only about the amount owed but also why and how the total was derived, and what kinds of payment plans are available. Remember, most patients don't understand all that is involved in a particular course of treatment, how health insurance works, or what all the items are on a billing statement. If patients don't understand the particulars, they won't trust the amount due. I'll talk later in this book about training employees in effective patient engagement. For now, let's focus on the price estimate and the importance of giving patients clear and detailed information about the services they will be receiving and the out-of-pocket costs that are involved. A complete, accurate, clear price estimate is more than a simple item of information for a patient. It is the foundation for building a relationship of trust that spans the entire healthcare encounter.

PATIENT PORTALS

According to a recent American Hospital Association Trend Watch report, the vast majority of patients are exchanging information about their health records over electronic tools like patient portals and EHRs. Ninety-two percent of patients contacted for the AHA report are now able to view their medical records online, far more than were able to do so two years before, when only 43 percent of patients said they could view their medical records online. The numbers of patients who can download their medical record information has increased from 30 percent to 84 percent in two years, and the number who can send the data to a third party rose six times. (10)

Some hospital administrators nevertheless are disappointed with the results generated by their payment portals. They expected that the vast majority of self-pay patients would pay online via portals, eliminating the costs of producing paper statements or the need to involve collection agencies.

Payment portals are, indeed, a relatively low-cost solution that's very appealing to providers: offer an online capability so patients can send payments for hospital services just as they pay other bills—one or two clicks and it's done.

Paying with a couple of clicks works for only some patients, however: those who have uncomplicated accounts and therefore have no questions and want a quick way to make what we call "unassisted payments." The problem for providers is that, unlike simple click purchases on Amazon or Wayfair, payment transactions for healthcare services are often highly complicated, covering several different clinical departments, procedures, and physician services, not to mention diagnostic and treatment codes. Additionally, insurance obligations and coverages often complicate the process. Many patients consequently need assistance before they feel comfortable doing the same. They'd like to know, for instance:

- Is the balance due before or after insurance?
- Do you realize I've already met my $1,500 deductible?
- Is this amount charged to me because I didn't have prior authorization?
- Will my payment be lower if the hospital appeals the denied claim?
- Do I qualify for financial assistance? Who do I talk to about that?
- Do I get a refund if insurance pays some or all of this amount?

These kinds of questions don't have simple yes or no answers, and they take time and effort to resolve by someone who fully understands the patient's situation and can provide chapter and verse.

It's certainly true that payment portals are an important component of good financial care; they require attention to detail. According to Avadyne data, to be successful, a patient portal needs to:

- Offer a personalized experience and user-designed interface
- Allow patients not only to make payments quickly but to combine bills and set up payment plans over a user-friendly platform
- Accept all types of payments and offer seamless financing options
- Provide mobile-friendly, secure transactions and links from the provider's website
- Incorporate high-quality training for staff (11)

Do remember though, a payment portal is only one way to keep the Slow Pay villain at bay. The Revenue Improver needs the other two allies—early access and price estimates—as well as a comprehensive Patient Concierge strategy. Forgive me for engaging in a little foreshadowing. You'll learn about that later.

In the past, providers would send out a few billing statements and then just forward unpaid accounts to collections. This did not create a positive reputation with communities and referral sources. Thankfully, the industry has come a long way.

At Mosaic, we are now looking at robust self-service options to increase patient satisfaction and limit the cost of customer service. Our populations are multigenerational. Millennials are tech-oriented and very sophisticated. Some elderly patients don't have a computer or smartphone and still prefer paper statements and correspondence, and as well, still write paper checks. We want to be able to accommodate all patients who require one-on-one engagement, while still moving self-service traffic toward technology.

We've taken the first step with our patient portal. Our goal is to have a bill portal where all charges combine into one statement. We refer to this as our "One-Bill" portal. We also have a medical record portal. We'll be combining both and adding artificial intelligence, so a patient can ask a question and AI will either traffic them to the right answer or send them to a customer service agent who's ready to respond.

Deborah Vancleave, Vice President of
Revenue Cycle, Mosaic Life Care

Complaints and Dissatisfaction

Two recent nationwide surveys found that patient satisfaction is closely tied to the patient's experience when paying for care and with the providers' payment processes.

A study of one thousand healthcare consumers conducted by Experian Health last September found that patients were most dissatisfied when it came to their dealings involving payment. Three specific issues topped the list of payment concerns that generated the most discontent: (1) the inability to fully comprehend the amount of money that patients owed for care; (2) how quoted out-of-pocket costs compared with fair market price; and (3) whether patients were financially able to pay for their care, Experian reported. Other key areas of dissatisfaction for patients were:

- "Determining what financial support is available,"
- "Ensuring that what is owed to the provider is accurate," and

- "Understanding the amount covered by their health insurance" (12)

A nationwide investigation conducted and reported last October by KVUE-TV, Austin, Texas, discovered that patients were concerned about the transparency of medical billing. Their complaints fell at both ends of the billing cycle: failure to provide clear and reasonable cost estimates upfront and failure to explain the bill afterward. This followed an earlier investigation by KVUE-TV after the station learned of a 1,000 percent increase in complaints to Texas Department of Insurance about balanced billing. The number of these complaints increased from 112 to 1,334 in three years' time. (13)

Illustrating the growing importance of patient satisfaction with providers' services on overall loyalty, a study by the healthcare communications company West showed that consumers are not afraid to leave an established relationship with a provider. Ninety percent of the patients in the survey said they would change providers if they were not completely satisfied, and 74 percent said they would delay scheduling an appointment or other kind of healthcare if they weren't satisfied with their provider. (14)

Captain Quantifier

These revenue cycle heroes and their teams can resolve complaints from patients and improve the Patient Financial Experience, which, in the end, will proactively improve liability and the cost to collect. Their tools?

1. Precise data collected regularly, monitored carefully, and used to measure and improve performance.

2. Scoring that lets providers track their performance over time, and to compare their performance with that of other similar institutions.

LACK OF DATA

As mentioned in the last chapter providers collect information on the patient experience, but this information concentrates on the clinical side of healthcare. HCAHPS surveys, you'll recall, collect patients' perceptions about the care they received in a hospital and focus on topics considered to be important to consumers. The results are compared across hospitals and they are publicly reported so data are widely accessible to payers and patients who are about to make decisions about healthcare.

You'll also recall that only two questions on the HCAHPS survey even remotely relate to the Patient Financial Experience: one asks about the patient's overall impression, the other whether the patient would recommend the hospital to others.

Although HCAHPS does not query patients about their financial experience specifically, the survey information directs providers' attention to patient satisfaction and how they can improve the patient's clinical experience. This, in turn, can lead to better financial performance. Experience has shown that consistent, high-level performance on HCAHPS helps providers bolster consumer loyalty, enhance their reputation in the marketplace, and increase referrals from satisfied patients. A positive clinical experience also has been found to reduce medical malpractice risk for physicians and staff turnover for providers. (15)

In addition, there are financial rewards for providers that score well on patient experience measures. Medicare's Hospital Value-Based Purchasing Program (VBP), for instance, links patient satisfaction to reimbursement; at least to some degree.

But what about the bottom line? Do high scores on patients' clinical experience mean better financial performance? It turns out this relationship has not been studied very much. In one of the few studies to explore this issue, the Deloitte Center for Health Solutions recently analyzed how HCAHPS scores affect measures of financial performance, such as net and operating margins and return on assets.

The Deloitte study concluded:

- Hospitals with high HCAHPS scores are more profitable. Hospitals with "excellent" HCAHPS patient ratings between 2008 and 2014 had a net margin of 4.7 percent, on average, as compared to just 1.8 percent for hospitals with "low" ratings.
- Providers that achieve a "top box" rating (9 or 10 out of a total score of 10 on HCAHPS) tend to have a 1.4 percent higher net margin and 1.3 percent increase in return on assets than those receiving a "bottom box" rating (0 to 6 out of a total score of 10).

"Faced with multiple priorities and resource demands," the study concluded, "health systems and hospitals may question the business value of collecting, analyzing, and acting upon patient experience data. However, these results suggest that good patient experience is associated with higher hospital profitability, and that this association is strongest for aspects of the patient experience most closely associated with better care (in particular, nurse-patient engagement)." (16)

Let me stress this: Findings from this study, and other experience, clearly demonstrate the value of providing a positive patient clinical experience. But this research still does not look directly at the patient's financial experience. Think what you can do with metrics that capture and quantify the patient's financial satisfaction!

Let me spend a little more time making the case for this kind of data.

THE NEED FOR PATIENT FINANCIAL SATISFACTION SCORES

There is no area of hospital operations that is so vital to the organization's existence than the patient's financial experience—and yet so little is really understood about it. It's a no-brainer: in order for providers to improve the Patient Financial Experience, complete—and trustworthy—data is necessary. But you know the story: surprisingly few hospitals have any of it. Even some of the most progressive and respected revenue cycle leaders I know admit they lack solid data on which to base important decisions. They do the best they can, knowing the information they rely on is flawed, misleading, or misses the point.

How do providers assess patient's financial satisfaction? As you've seen with HCAHPS, providers try to wean out data that may be important for financial performance from organization-wide general satisfaction metrics. Not only are survey responses largely irrelevant to the Patient Financial Experience, they provide only a small glimpse into patient satisfaction, if any at all. The overall response rate from patients to the HCAHPS survey is only 30 percent. Relating HCAHPS information to the Patient Financial Experience amounts to a spotty afterthought.

Even when providers examine the financial side of the patient experience, more often than not, they look at the experiences of a small fraction of their patients—those who respond to random calls or call in themselves with complaints. Now don't get me wrong, it's important to study patient complaints (we'll get into that later). But basing decisions on "outlier" information? Not a very good move.

Quality assurance as it's typically done in the revenue cycle is limited and labor intensive. Auditors get down into the weeds:

Did the employee greet the patient by name, get specific items of information, and end the patient encounter with: Is there anything more I can help you with today? Decisions rely too heavily on bad news from individual patients. I've known revenue cycle leaders who have made changes in their processes after a single call or complaint reached the CEO's office.

Just consider all the information that's missed when a provider reviews only a handful of patient interactions. Underlying and pervasive problems can be totally overlooked. Worse, providers may get the false impression that everything is hunky dory.

Wouldn't it be much better to take all revenue cycle interactions into account? To review all the calls, bills, texts, and social media encounters across the full spectrum of revenue cycle encounters? Only then can a provider get a spot-on picture of whether patients are having a world-class experience or a subpar one.

Wouldn't it be much better to use the information gathered about the Patient Financial Experience to help revenue cycle staff prevent problems from occurring? To deescalate and resolve issues before they turn into complaints and dissatisfaction?

DEESCALATION

In contrast to the clinical side of the patient experience (which has a dizzying array of metrics for tracking and measures the processes that lead to good outcomes—and can be used to intercede and prevent complaints and complications), the revenue cycle is not designed to operate as proactively. In most cases it can be challenging to know which patients are at high-risk for having a poor financial outcome and which are likely to resort to escalation.

But just as there are symptoms or factors in the patient medical history that can be used to place patients into high-risk categories for less-than-optimal clinical outcome, there are well-known factors which place patients at high risk for a poor financial outcome. What a game changer for complaint management in the revenue cycle: winnowing out the signs of escalation from the full array of data obtained from patient encounters. Revenue cycle staff then have an opportunity to prevent an unhappy patient from:

- Telling others about the poor experience. If this colors the attitude of just one person, it could mean lost revenue for the provider.
- Posting on social media. This could hit a nerve with many people in a community who already are predisposed to think that providers are only out for money.
- Contacting local news. No matter how the story turns out, it's negative press that can seriously damage the provider's reputation.
- Venting frustration to a hospital leader.

The revenue cycle leader is the last person standing between a disgruntled and a satisfied patient, the last one who can answer the question: What is going wrong here and what can I do to get back on the right track?

THE RIGHT KIND OF DATA

So what do providers need to do? Become a hero—a Captain Quantifier—by taking these steps:

1. Collect information about all complaints associated with the Patient Financial Experience, not only the formal written complaints, but everyday interactions. If a registrar overhears a patient say she doesn't think it's right for the hospital to collect money in the ER, or

a hospitalized patient thinks she's too sick to discuss payment plans or, while handing over a credit card for payment, a patient mutters: "Wish I'd known sooner that I was going to have to fork over all this money." All of these are complaints and should be logged and acted upon.

2. Examine all encounters. Quality assurance in the revenue cycle usually reviews a sample of patient encounters, maybe ten out of one hundred calls made. Although the calls are examined carefully, the process overlooks a large number of patient interactions. Valuable information will not be gathered, and opportunities for improvement lost.

3. Intervene before a problem intensifies, not after-the-fact. So, what? We're asking you to rub magic stones together and get a glimpse of the future? No, definitely not. Analytics are what will help you take proactive ownership of your patient encounter data.

SCORING

Think of complaints as an opportunity because they can drive change. Think also about broadening the definition of a complaint in the revenue cycle. Certain aspects of the revenue cycle are associated with an increased risk for patient dissatisfaction. These can serve as criteria for measuring change, such as new or corrected insurance, account information after initial bill or the time it takes to send the first patient bill after completion of hospital service.

By breaking complaints down into their constituent parts, you can acknowledge the issue, focus analysis on root causes, plan corrective action, monitor the results, and score performance over a period of months.

Here's how that might look:

Criteria	Feedback	Action
New or corrected insurance or account information	• Eighteen percent of accounts indicate account errors • Eighty-two percent of accounts indicate new insurance info found	1. Review account for missing/incorrect adjustments 2. Review insurance eligibility preservice process 3. Review type of account (i.e., ER vs. scheduled, etc.)
Time from hospital service to first patient bill	• Twenty-seven percent of accounts aged greater than ninety days from discharge to first statement	1. Review billing processes 2. Review clean claim rate 3. Review claim to payment 4. Review payment to first statement

With this kind of information, you can begin generating scores for each criterion each month and an overall score across the revenue cycle.

The next step is to analyze factors that predict patient behavior. Speech analytics technology is an effective tool.

SPEECH ANALYTICS

Speech analytics software has been around for more than fifteen years. Its use has grown widely in many industries because of its accuracy and quick return of intelligence on customers. In a nutshell, speech analytics software analyzes conversations made over the telephone, by email, social media, text, or web chats; then transcribes all of the content of the conversations and turns it into data that can be searched.

Speech analytics match raw data from conversations with desired items of information that can be structured for later scoring, including the person who handled the call, time of day, length of call, etc. Speech recognition transforms sounds into text and flags acoustic signals of agitation, including changes in the pitch of the voice, the speed of speech, periods of silence or loudness. Language and other metrics are then combined into a score that can be coupled with performance indicators of consumer satisfaction, etc. (17)

Putting It All Together

With speech analytics revenue cycle heroes can accumulate information on the factors that trigger patient dissatisfaction, link these factors to revenue cycle criteria, and produce an evidence-based score on patient satisfaction. This scoring information can be tallied on an ongoing basis to produce a report card on performance as well as objective and accurate feedback for monitoring and training.

When you think about the process clinicians follow to identify high-risk patients and compare this to the tools available for revenue cycle leaders (like none), you realize it's time to take a page out of the evidence-based clinical playbook and apply it to financial interactions with patients. Like clinicians—who don't have to guess which patients are at higher risk for a poor surgical outcome because they have data to tell them—revenue cycle leaders can follow a similar, evidence-based model to discover how patients feel about the way a hospital treated them financially. There's no guesswork here or crystal ball-gazing. With actual data on who's satisfied, who isn't, and why, revenue cycle leaders can predict what the patient's loyalty or actions are going to be. That's valuable information in and of itself, but the best part is, it can be used to train revenue cycle staff to respond in real-time situations.

As heroes move along in their Journey, Christopher Vogler writes in *The Writer's Journey*, they "are wise to make themselves as ready as they'll ever be, like warriors polishing and sharpening their weapons or students doing final drills before a big exam." (18)

In the second part of the *Maze Runner* saga, Thomas and his fellow Gladers face their greatest challenge. They must search for information about the mysterious and powerful organization known as WCKD. Their journey takes them to the Scorch, a desolate locale with unimaginable obstacles, where they team up with resistance fighters and mobilize against WCKD.

Newt: We're with you, Thomas.

Minho: Do it, Thomas.

Frypan: We're ready.

Thomas: We're not going back there. It's the only way.
The Scorch Trials, 20th Century Fox, 2015 (19)

Questions & Considerations

- How well-trained are your preservice staff to have Patient Financial Experience conversations?

- Do preservice staff have the tools they need to provide a great Patient Financial Experience?

- What elements does your price estimation tool consider? Does it calculate estimates based on insurance contract modeling?

- Does it calculate estimates based on historical payments from similar types of patients?

- Does it consider the patient's deductible, co-insurance, and out-of-pocket costs?

- Do you have a patient portal?

- Does your patient portal facilitate answering patients' questions about their account or billing statement?

- Do you have any means of predicting patient complaints or escalations?

CHAPTER 6

The Journey Continues

In their path from the Ordinary to the New World heroes often stumble, believing the trip is too long, the trials and tribulations too onerous. They begin to doubt: Why do we need to change? We've been getting along. Okay, it's not great, but it's what we know how to do. Why now? What's the rush? This is just too hard. It takes too much energy. I don't know enough to get this done. Yet they persevere, build competence in areas where it is lacking, learn from mentors, coaches, and peers, and move forward, even if it's step by step.

> **Steve Trevor:** This is no man's land, Diana! It means no man can cross it, all right? This battalion has been here for nearly a year and they've barely gained an inch. All right? Because on the other side there are a bunch of Germans pointing machine guns at every square inch of this place. This is not something you can cross. It's not possible.
>
> **Diana Prince:** So…what? So we do nothing?

Steve Trevor: No, we are doing something! We are! We just…
we can't save everyone in this war. This is not what we came
here to do.

Diana Prince: No. But it's what I'm going to do.
Wonder Woman, Warner Brothers, 2017 (1)

To continue on the Hero's Journey, revenue cycle leaders need
to shuck off the attitudes that may be holding them back and realize
yes, they do need to change. Their organizations haven't been getting
along all that well. The time for change is now, and yes, they can do it.

In this chapter we'll look at villains that threaten the revenue
cycle: Ineffective Training and Cost to Collect and the hero behaviors
that can put these rapscallions in their place: Revenue Super Coach
and Patient Satisfaction Champion.

Ineffective Training

"I am furious about the way I've been treated by this hospital." This
is the first thing a hospital's CEO hears when an irate caller is put
through to his office early one morning. And, unfortunately, the
patient's comment—and his experience—occur far more often than
providers would like to think.

"Sir," the unhappy caller continues, "my family and I have been
coming to your hospital for years. My wife had all of our children
there. My grandchildren were born there. My surgeon practices there.
But it's as if none of you in that institution knows a thing about us!"

"I am so sorry, sir," the CEO says. "Please tell me what's hap-
pened, beginning with your name."

"That's more courtesy than that…that…debt collector of yours
could muster. I mean, calling me the day before my surgery and asking
for five thousand dollars. Just like that. It felt like, 'Pay up, old man, or

you don't get your operation.' And your representative didn't even get my name right or take the time to explain about our deductible. We thought we had already met the deductible. We didn't know how much this operation was going to cost—at least how much it was going to cost me. I never...ever...got an estimate. This is how you treat your patients?"

Later the same day, the man's daughter tweets about the incident and a local news reporter hops on it. He's been working on a story about high-deductible health plans and what they mean for patients who need healthcare. In no time the man and his family are headliners on the evening news.

The initial angry call didn't come out of nowhere, did it? This patient certainly did not plan to be dialing the CEO's number. (Nor did he ever consider talking to a local TV reporter—he's always been camera shy, for goodness sake!) So how did this happen?

Let's go back to the beginning of this relationship story. Over the years the man came to depend on this hospital. After all, it's been there for him, for his wife and children, his friends and loved ones. Now it's his turn: he has a serious medical condition and everyone agrees he needs life-saving surgery. In his time of need he is comforted that he can seek healthcare in a familiar place, in this hospital, where, he's certain, the clinical team has him covered.

And payment? That shouldn't be a problem. The man has the same insurance he's always had, from his long-term employer. His wife's appendectomy was fully covered a few months back, he remembers, so he has no reason to think about money. Besides, nobody at the hospital ever said anything to him about payment.

After his presurgical testing and the blood work come back okay and he gets detailed instructions about how to prevent infection and prepare for surgery, which he's following to the letter, the only thing he's thinking about the day before surgery is making sure the neighbor can walk his dog in the morning and there's plenty of gas in the car to get to the hospital at 5:00 a.m.

The man finally gets to sleep—very early because the alarm clock is set for 3:00 a.m.—when the phone rings. It's someone from the hospital, he realizes, although he can't quite make out the woman's name, who's saying something about a five thousand dollar balance that's due. He isn't able to follow much of what the person is saying—something about a deductible and an out-of-pocket maximum.

Next, the man hears something about actual liability, and he suddenly realizes he could be on the hook for as much as sixty-thousand dollars since an operating room costs one thousand dollars a minute. That's the same amount as the down payment on his house! The man balks and challenges the woman. "What do you mean? What are you talking about?" he sputters. "Why haven't I heard anything about this before?"

"Well, you know," the woman on the phone says, "it's important to check your insurance coverage before you scheduled the surgery, then you could have known."

The conversation goes downhill fast. The man's wife gets on the phone, upset. "Surely there must be some mistake." The person on the other end of the line (whose name neither the man nor his wife can recall later), mumbles something about perhaps they should reschedule the surgery if they can't come up with the money.

The patient, who was asleep just minutes before, is now wide awake and angry. Taking the telephone receiver from his wife, he demands to know why he wasn't notified about the need for payment until the day before his surgery, then slams down the phone. Turning to his wife, he asks: "What are we going to do?"

Regardless of what happens next—whether the patient pays the five thousand dollars and has the surgery, or chooses to seek medical care elsewhere—one thing's for certain. That man will never forget the experience he had with the hospital. He will never understand all the factors that came into play: the fact that his employer over the last year selected a less expensive, high-deductible, healthcare insurance plan to allow employees and the employer to save money on premiums but exposed them to high out-of-pocket costs. Nor will he appreciate the hospital's long record of corporate philanthropy nor the millions of dollars of charity care it provides. The hospital wasn't there for him when he needed it. He won't go there again—he won't make that mistake again.

Who's the villain here? Ineffective Training. Who can put that villain out of commission? You got it: A Revenue Cycle Super Coach.

Revenue Super Coach

With her X-ray glasses, what would Revenue Super Coach see when she looks at this situation?

- First, no one talked to the patient about money until the day before surgery. Aha, the superhero realizes: Front-end staff need training on how to facilitate early financial account clearance.
- Second, the staff person was not empathetic, kind, or friendly. Instead, the caller blamed the patient for failing to do something the patient had no idea he was supposed to do. All staff need customer service training geared specifically toward the Patient Financial Experience.
- Third, the staff person could not explain how the total amount of the surgery was calculated. Staff need training on how to discuss often complex specifics about health insurance—and how they relate to each individual patient—as well as hospital charges.

Developing Great Communicators

You realize, of course, the revenue cycle role bears little resemblance to what it was just a few years ago. It's gotten far more complicated, with many new skill sets required. It's difficult to name a role in healthcare that has changed more significantly, in fact, than that of the revenue cycle employee. Front-end staff now need to be able to accurately verify insurance coverage, understand how all kinds of factors affect a patient's liability, have complex financial discussions with patients, and collect patient liability upfront in various care settings. Revenue cycle staff are interacting with clinical colleagues if orders are missing or incomplete. They're obtaining countless more authorizations and in shorter timeframes than in the past. They're even getting involved when claims are denied inappropriately by insurers, and keeping track of ever-changing requirements on payer websites. Revenue cycle employees have a lot on their plates, to say the least. To make things even more challenging, staff need to deliver a very high level of customer service during often complex, sometimes problematic, and occasionally confrontational interactions.

Great financial communication doesn't happen by chance. And it shouldn't be an isolated occurrence. Many revenue cycle leaders talk proudly about their "star collectors" or their "go-to registrar"—about employees who seem to have a knack for turning even the tensest situations around or for putting a smile on a patient's face even as she's paying a sizeable hospital bill. But no matter how much of a "people person" these employees may be, the fact is, financial experiences encompass more than just one interaction, sometimes many more. Even if the patient is lucky enough to encounter one of these "service stars," the next encounter—or the one before it—might be so poor that it casts a negative light on the overall experience. Good financial care, like good clinical care, is not a one-off. It's a series of encounters, and each one needs to be part of a world-class experience.

If most revenue cycle leaders are honest, they'll acknowledge that some of their employees have difficulty handling complex financial conversations about high-dollar liability. Trying to provide enough training to these employees, in order to avoid complaints and dissatisfaction, is straining the limited resources of many departments. But training is an investment that pays for itself over and over. To put it another way, there's no difficult financial interaction that can't be helped with good training. The opposite is also true: Any financial interaction, even a simple co-pay collection, can escalate because of poor training. For ANY financial encounter, training is always a factor. Every time a revenue cycle employee interacts with a patient, the hospital's investment in training, or lack thereof, is on display.

Overall, in fact, I believe training plays an even bigger part in how satisfied patients ultimately are. Without it, I've seen how even the simplest conversation can go haywire. With it, even a serious situation can get back on track, with a solution found. Not everyone is a born customer-service star. But we've found training strategies anyone can use to improve satisfaction when having financial conversations.

So what are some elements of effective customer service training for the revenue cycle?

FIRST STEPS: THE GREETING

A warm, sincere greeting using a person's name—with plenty of eye contact when speaking face-to-face—is an excellent start. But financial conversations can go off the rails soon after "hello" if employees aren't well-trained. Granted, not everyone is a customer-service natural. Some people have to work a little harder to "get it." But everyone can improve satisfaction with some proven techniques to avoid escalation and improve the odds that the patient engagement is positive and the patient, if not happy, at least is not dissatisfied.

Here are some other things Revenue Super Coach has found to be helpful after years of training hundreds of revenue cycle employees:

ACTIVE LISTENING

Think of a person you know—a friend or family member—someone you tell all your troubles to. That person's a great listener. Well, those very same skills are what's needed for a world-class financial conversation. Sometimes things are left unsaid by the patient. Other times, the patient can't stop talking because of the need to vent. That's where active listening comes in. It's a process which allows an employee to pick up on the clues that someone's worried—really worried—about money. Maybe the patient knew he had a high-deductible plan and he hadn't planned on needing to schedule surgery so soon. Maybe he wished he'd sprung for the better coverage but simply couldn't afford it.

In my experience most people who go into healthcare are caring people. They want to offer world-class customer service. When they learn how to be active listeners, they suddenly can. Even when a patient is upset, the employee who's been trained as an active listener doesn't just listen to what the patient is saying but hears the message, like the patient cannot afford another high-interest loan. The employee then realizes she has something to offer—a no-interest loan with very low, monthly payments. The employee allows the patient to vent, waits for a break in the conversation, and says, "We do have a payment option I can help you with today, to eliminate paying any interest."

There's something interesting that we hear all the time from front-end staff. They tell us that training not only allows them to do a better job, but it also positively impacts their relationships with family and friends, too. It turns out that, in life and it's certainly true with financial discussions, active listening offers a huge advantage.

TAILORED TALK

Some people love to make small talk and love an employee who engages in some pleasant conversation about her vacation—or their own. Others want just the facts and appreciate a well-prepared employee who's gone over the numbers very carefully before picking up the phone to call the patient. Well-trained revenue cycle employees need to know which approach is best.

NO ZEROS

Phrases like, "We can't," quite simply never help matters. Instead, we use "hero" phrases: "Here's what I can do for you." If the patient says she can pay ten dollars a month, and the employee knows the minimum is twenty-five dollars, that employee doesn't say, "You cannot pay ten dollars a month because it does not meet our minimum." The employee says, "What I can do today is set this up at twenty-five dollars a month." By avoiding negative words, the interaction stays positive.

BASIC KNOWLEDGE

Employees shouldn't even collect a fifty dollar co-pay if they can't explain how they came up with the amount. Why not? Simple—it's the patient's money we are talking about. Patients who owe significant amounts might need to make some hard decisions about whether to deplete their emergency savings fund or borrow money from a family member. With patients going through scenarios like that in their minds, the employee better have the numbers correct.

ROLE PLAYING

Imagine having a tough conversation about money with a total stranger. This person could go absolutely berserk, blame you, resort to profanity, or burst into tears. Since all this and more is going to happen sometime—it's all in a day's work for the revenue cycle—employees need to role play. This gives everyone a chance to come up with the best possible arsenal of responses. If a patient says she was quoted a lower amount by someone else, for instance, stating, "Well, I don't know who would have told you THAT," causes numerous problems. The patient may find a reason to complain about the other department the first chance she gets. By role playing employees can catch inflammatory responses like these before they are inappropriately used with patients.

Service Recovery

No matter how well trained revenue cycle staff are, there are bound to be situations that do not go as well as expected. When things do go bad, revenue cycle leaders may follow the approach outlined in *Exceptional Service, Exceptional Profit* by Leonardo Inghilleri and Micah Solomon: First apologize, then review the issue with patient. Fix the problem so the patient no longer feels wronged or let down and add something extra. Provide quick follow-up to show concern and any progress that is being made and follow up again after the problem has been resolved to reinforce for the patient that the revenue cycle is there to help. Be sure to report the problem and how it was resolved so the revenue cycle can not only document the incident but also link it to any other similar incidents, identify trends in performance, and track overall patient satisfaction.

As Solomon points out, every company needs to have a framework for addressing lapses in customer service. For Starbuck's, it's LATTE: Listen to the customer, Acknowledge the problem, Take action, Thank the customer, and Explain what was done. (2) For Marriott, it's LEARN: Listen. Empathize. Apologize. Respond. Notify.

Solomon's own system for customer service recovery is AWARE:

- Acknowledge the situation, apologize immediately and sincerely. The objective is to recognize the customer's situation and express regret for what he or she has experienced. A key is to understand and share the customer's perspective.
- Widen understanding about the situation. Ask questions to determine exactly why the customer is upset and explain his or her viewpoint. Recognize that the customer's opinions may differ or reveal an entirely new issue. Involve the customer in finding a solution that works for him or her.
- Agree with the customer on the proposed solution to the problem and make a commitment to take specific steps in a specific time frame.
- Resolve to take care of the situation as agreed upon, follow-up with people who are responsible for making corrections, and get back with the customer to make sure all is well.
- Evaluate the entire process. Report the situation and its resolution in the customer's profile and incorporate the information in the organizational quality control process. Assess the issue and its resolution to find and correct systemic problems, learn from the experience, and make it part of future and ongoing staff training.

The AWARE system can be used to form the core of a patient financial concierge service (see Chapter 8) that will keep revenue cycle staff attuned to patients' needs. Remember, when your revenue cycle employee has to explain to a patient that he owes thousands of dollars and needs to pay, it's crucial to make this conversation one of the best customer service experiences the patient has ever had. The memory of paying the money will fade, but the feeling the revenue cycle employee provided—of undivided attention and world-class service—won't soon be forgotten. And, when that patient writes a complimentary letter or posts on social media about it, the revenue cycle leader, CEO, and hospital board won't soon forget.

At each point of contact with a patient, we have a "happen kit" so if something doesn't go right with registration or scheduling issues, our employees are empowered to make it right with them. If we miss something or there's a problem, the employees are able to give a gift certificate or gas card or even a voucher for a night in a hotel.

As CFO I was worried that this would be an open-ended deal and we would go through the money right and left. But this doesn't get used that often. So we're talking about hundreds of dollars a year, not thousands, and it helps defuse difficult situations and turns a negative into a positive or at least prevents a negative.

Dave Muhs, Chief Financial Officer,
Henry County Health Center

Cost to Collect

Collections was the top issue identified by healthcare CFOs in a 2015 survey conducted by the Healthcare Financial Management Association. Hardly a surprise since collections is one of the costliest administrative function in a hospital. (3)

Collections has changed significantly in the last few years. There has been some good news and some bad. The Affordable Care Act was expected to provide access to healthcare insurance coverage to about thirty million uninsured individuals and in the process reduce bad debt for providers. Indeed, the uninsured rate among adults fell by nearly 6 percent between 2013 and 2017. (4)

The shift in bad debt from uninsured self-pay patients to covered individuals as a result increased the likelihood that providers would receive at least some payment. It also, however, meant an increase in Balances After Insurance (BAI), which require more effective and efficient methods of collection. Collecting BAI, by necessity, focuses on interactions with individual patients and involves more hands-on work and yet it produces lower overall collected amounts. The Advisory Board estimates each collection from a patient costs an average of twenty-five dollars, and McKinsey and Company reports that providers collect only 50 to 70 percent of a patient's BAI. (5–6)

On top of that, revenue cycle operations can be notoriously inefficient. Claims processing, payments, billing, etc., account for fifteen cents of every healthcare dollar spent in the U.S. Compare this to the retail industry, where payment transaction costs account for only two cents for every retail transaction and one cent for every automated retail payment transaction. (7)

Despite the need for improved IT systems, revenue cycle management tends to fall to the bottom of the priority list when it comes to upgrades. According to a Black Book survey, 48 percent of CFOs are concerned that organizational budgets will prevent them from upgrading revenue cycle software. (8)

The Patient Satisfaction Champion

Revenue cycle leaders can benefit by taking a different look at collection fees—unbundling self-pay patient accounts, categorizing them not only by patients' ability or propensity to pay, but also by the number and type of services they need to pay. Are they do-it-yourself payers or do they need to reach out and talk with someone?

Younger generations clearly are more comfortable with, and use technology and social media more than older generations. According to Pew Research Center, nearly all Millennials (92 percent) and GenXers (85 percent) own a smartphone. Baby Boomers? Sixty-five percent. And those born before 1945? Only 30 percent.

The story is similar for social media. Eighty-five percent of Millennials and 75 percent of GenXers are on social media, while Facebook, Twitter, Snapchat, etc., are used by only 57 percent of Boomers and 23 percent of older individuals. (9)

From this information, you would think younger generations would be more likely to welcome self-service healthcare payment options and require no assistance when it comes to making payments. However, Avadyne's recent research contradicts this assumption:

- Older generations require less assistance (self-service) AND pay more. Less than 30 percent of Baby Boomers and older individuals require assistance when paying healthcare bills. And both groups end up paying upward of 70 percent of their bills.
- Younger generations pay less and require more assistance. Millennials and GenXers pay about 60 percent of their bills and 35 percent need assistance when paying.

These differences can be explained by experience with the healthcare system. Older individuals tend to stick with the same providers for years. They consequently have a high degree of trust in their providers. Their insurance coverage is less complex, and they have been dealing with healthcare insurance for years. (10)

Younger people tend to switch providers more often and therefore do not have the chance to develop trust. Their insurance coverage is more complicated, and they have had few encounters with the healthcare system or payment.

This analysis shows that:

- For every dollar collected, younger generations have a higher cost to collect than older generations for healthcare payments.
- Patients want self-service…but many, particularly younger individuals, need assistance.

It's no wonder then that one out of two patients in our Bridging the Gap survey said they want a dedicated concierge (support person) to engage with them throughout their financial experience. I'll explain more about a Patient Financial Concierge approach in chapter 8.

Diana Prince: [dances with Steve] Is this what people do when there are no wars to fight?

Steve Trevor: Yeah…this, and other things.

Diana Prince: What things?

Steve Trevor: Um, they have breakfast. They love their breakfast. And, um, they love to wake up and read the paper and go to work, they get married, make some babies, grow up together. I guess.

Diana Prince: What is that like?

Steve Trevor: I have no idea.
Wonder Woman, Warner Brothers, 2017 (12)

Questions & Considerations

- What training do you have available to your team?

- Is there a consistent, stepped communication approach with patients?

- Do you have a documented Service Recovery process?

- Do customer service representatives understand what they are empowered to do to resolve a customer service issue?

- Do you have scripting for common conversations?

- Do you have role playing as a part of training?

- Do you understand the impact of generations and their actions in your revenue cycle?

CHAPTER 7

Transformation

Teenager Wade Watts lives with his aunt in one of the trailer homes
that are stacked on top of each other in a poverty-stricken area
that emerged after the energy and overpopulation crises of the 2040s.
Like everyone else in this world, Watts spends most of his time in the
OASIS, a virtual society he accesses with a visor and haptic gloves.
The OASIS is far more than an escape; it is an all-encompassing world
that promises wealth and fame: Find the three keys and unlock the
Easter egg that lies within the virtual world and inherit the entire
fortune of OASIS' creator James Halliday, as well as ownership of
his company, Gregarious Games, Inc.

> **Wade:** These days, reality is a bummer. Everyone is looking for a
> way to escape, and that's why Halliday was such a hero to us. He
> showed us that we could go somewhere without going anywhere
> at all. You don't need a destination when you're running on an
> omnidirectional treadmill with quadraphonic, pressure-sensitive
> underlay. James Halliday saw the future. And then he built it.
> He gave us a place to go. A place called the OASIS, a place
> where the limits of reality are your own imagination. You can

do anything, go anywhere. Like the vacation planet. Surf a fifty-foot monster wave in Hawaii. You can ski down the pyramids. You can climb Mount Everest with Batman. Check out this place. It's a casino the size of a planet. You can lose your money there. You can get married. You can get divorced. People come to the OASIS for all the things they can do, but they stay because of all the things they can be. Tall, beautiful, scary, a different sex, a different species, live-action, cartoon. It's all your call." *Ready Player One*, Warner Brothers Pictures, 2018 (1)

This is the time when the hero faces the greatest challenge, the point when he changes or transforms, when he applies the new rules or weapons he learned during the previous phase of the Hero's Journey, when he realizes the trick or insight he gained to thwart his enemies in the past prepares him for entering The New World.

> **Creator of the virtual society OASIS, James Halliday:** [In the form of my avatar, Anorak the All Knowing] I created three keys. Three hidden keys open three secret gates
> Wherein the errant will be tested for worthy traits
> And those with the skill to survive these straits
> Will reach The End where the prize awaits" (1)

Revenue cycle leaders on their own Hero's Journey have many ways to prepare for The New World. One of the most exciting involves emerging digital technology known as augmented reality.

Augmented Reality—What It Is

Augmented reality superimposes graphics, audio, and other sensory enhancements on top of a real-world environment in real time. It's already common on televised broadcasts drawing first-down lines on the football field while the game is in progress, and it's being used in industry to visualize and repair machinery, maintain equipment from a distance or in remote, hard-to-otherwise reach locales, handle dangerous chemicals or tasks. (2)

According to Apple, augmented reality in the iOS is being used by many major corporations: American Airlines is developing a system that will help travelers navigate unfamiliar airports. IKEA has an app that allows potential buyers to bring their new furniture home, virtually, and see it in their living room. Other companies have AR systems that allow physicians and surgeons to delve into and around the human body, biologists to examine anatomy without dissection, students to experience subject matter as if it were first-hand, and games players to enter and interact with an alternative society, like *Ready Player One's* OASIS. (3)

At the present time AR systems display graphics from only one point of view for the entire audience. Next generation systems will display graphics for each viewer's perspective. Research labs around the world are working on AR systems that utilize simple, off-the-shelf equipment, such as a camera, small projector, smartphone, and mirror, to examine the surrounding world, focus on an image and process it, gather information from the internet, and project that information onto the surface in front of the user. (4)

While the AR market is already robust—with steady demand from the automotive, fashion, and manufacturing sectors—it is expected to grow exponentially in the next few years. A recent market analysis projects a combined average annual growth rate of 39 percent, making AR a $30 billion industry by 2023. (5)

Why Organizations Need AR

Harvard Professor Michael E. Porter and industrial software producer James E. Heppelmann recently concluded that every business and organization should have a strategy for incorporating and applying AR to increase productivity and enhance value. Reporting in *Harvard*

Business Review, the authors wrote: "combining the capabilities of machines with humans' distinctive strengths will lead to far greater productivity and more value creation than either could generate alone. What's needed to realize this opportunity is a powerful human interface that bridges the gap between the digital and physical worlds. We see AR as a historic innovation that provides this interface. It helps humans enhance their own capabilities by taking advantage of new digital knowledge and machine capabilities. It will profoundly change training and skill development, allowing people to perform sophisticated work without protracted and expensive conventional instruction—a model that is inaccessible to so many today, AR, then, enables people to better tap into the digital revolution and all it has to offer." (6)

AR in Medicine

Unlike virtual reality, whose 3-D world is detached from the user, AR keeps users in touch with reality. It also sends information to the eyes in lightning speed. As an article in *Medical Futurist* explained recently, these two properties make the technology ideal for use in medicine. In the next three to five years AR will be standard equipment for emergency responders in the field, surgeons in the OR, and nurses at the bedside. It will help patients better describe their symptoms and allow drug companies to explain the dosages, side effects, and best ways for patients to take their medications. (7)

But that's a glimpse of the future. Let's see how AR can be used today—in the revenue cycle.

AR and the Healthcare Bill

A patient receives a hospital bill in the mail. What happens next is legend. The puzzling document full of numbers and annotations that look like they need a team of CPAs and lawyers to decipher falls to the floor, the patient slaps a palm on her forehead, and shakes her head in frustration. "Now, what am I supposed to do?" she asks.

The healthcare industry has struggled for more than twenty years to develop a billing statement that is easy to understand. Even the simplest, most attractive billing statement still has an amount due, and patients often have questions about it. Sometimes the questions are easy to answer, and sometimes they are very complex. Technology could provide an answer here. Its importance in healthcare financial education is steadily increasing. But the healthcare industry is struggling there, too. A whopping 89 percent of consumers under the age of 40 were dissatisfied with the technology capabilities of their healthcare organization, according to an April 2018 Black Book Research survey. (8)

But there is a way to innovate with technology, streamline the healthcare billing statement, improve satisfaction of the Patient Financial Experience, and keep human resources costs down. Yes, it's through augmented reality.

AN AUGMENTED REALITY AVATAR

Let's imagine an augmented reality (AR) avatar—a 3-D digital concierge—who pops up on top of a billing statement and walks across the columns and numbers, explaining bits of it as she moves along. The goal here is to provide anticipatory customer service as the AR avatar answers some basic questions, such as, "Does this bill take into account the fact that I've already met my deductible?" or "How much did my insurance company pay?"

The avatar (Eve, her name is) covers questions about billing (and in a visually enticing, fun way). Eve explains when payment on the bill is due and how much is owed. She also shows patients how to pay online through a single-touch digital access directly to a payment portal, contact a financial concierge by phone or email, and find important hospital links. (And, she'll soon be covering a lot more.)

Eve does, indeed, anticipate customer needs—in this case, questions about a hospital bill—but not by reading a patient's mind. She's actually making smart use of what revenue cycle staff know from experience are the questions patients most likely have about their bills. By answering them digitally, Eve saves patients from making a telephone call or a trip to the hospital to get answers to straightforward questions. A win for the patient and for the hospital.

Now a patient will have a targeted question or two. But instead of "What do all these numbers mean?" the patient could drill down to ask, "Is there anything I can do about the portion of the bill the insurance is denying as a noncovered service?" Or, "It seems that insurance has already paid what they're going to pay. I can't pay the $2,100 balance. What options do I have?"

Two things are possible with the avatar model. One: all the patient's questions are answered so there are no remaining barriers to payment. There's no further need for phone calls or in-person meetings. The patient can move on to pay the hospital bill and resolve liability with a quick trip to the payment portal. The result: account resolution plus a satisfied patient.

Two: the patient still needs to understand some aspect of billing and/or payment. It turns out that for this patient, the avatar concierge helped somewhat, but not enough to move on to payment; the questions were more complex than the avatar could handle.

Was the avatar a waste of time in this case? Not at all. The avatar cleared up at least some of the confusion so the patient is more in-the-know about the financial situation. She knows insurance has already paid its part and the deductible has been factored into the bill amount. She can now focus on issues such as why and what can be done now?

The avatar is one part of an overall financial education interaction that can give patients valuable information without requiring a series of labor-intensive staff explanations or increasing the cost to collect.

But there is another more intangible benefit to the avatar concierge—being on the forefront of a blossoming new technology. Let's not underestimate the impact of technology on financial satisfaction. We know very well that consumers choose providers based on how up-to-date their clinical technology is. That's why hospitals acquire wide-bore MRIs and 3-D mammograms and promote them in the marketplace.

But hospitals seem to have a blind spot when it comes to technology for billing practices. We've already reviewed how clinical satisfaction is analyzed, measured, and tracked—with publicly reported quality measures driving the measurement—and how satisfaction drives patient loyalty. Well, the same is true for technology on the clinical and administrative side. The Black Book survey shows that 84 percent of consumers seek out the most technologically-advanced and electronically-communicative medical organizations. (8)

I would go so far as to say, frustration with outmoded technology residing solely in the financial services area can drive consumers away even if they're happy with the clinical care they receive. The conventional wisdom is that clinical care is the patient's priority and financial care places a distant second, if it's factored in at all. In fact, good financial care can be a key driver in attracting consumers to a hospital, and for today's patient, that means having the right kind of technology in the right place at the right time.

It makes sense. What if your favorite hotel didn't have a website for online reservations? Or if the online reservation system had annoying glitches, such as offering room categories that weren't actually available? Chances are, you'd consider staying somewhere that made reservations easy. It's also true with everyday bills. Some utility companies make it possible to pay the bill just by sending a text message. A consumer who is used to this will not favorably view a competitor that requires a lengthy online form to make a payment.

It's not too soon to think about this. We're already seeing examples of augmented reality in the consumer world. Recently, an Australian winery brought the story of its brand to life with a talking label, made possible with AR. Those kinds of experiences, where technology interacts with the consumer to tell stories or answer questions before the consumer thinks to ask them, are going to become commonplace because they're fun and edgy even as they inform.

Healthcare billing statements will never be as interesting or fun as the labels on bottles of wine. However, there's absolutely no reason why they can't be a heck of a lot more pleasant and interactive. The look of the billing statement is a relatively easy fix. But providers can go well beyond appearance and put smart technology to work to improve the Patient Financial Experience.

Receiving and paying for healthcare services can be a confusing experience. Patients often don't understand clinical and revenue cycle terms and topics and they haven't had a place to go to easily get that information and be educated on what is a diagnosis, procedures, protocols, co-pay, coinsurance, claim adjudication, or understand an EOB.

We're implementing ways of providing some of that educational content for our customers to access at home or at a Banner facility. We're starting in the revenue cycle, but believe there is room to expand to topics such as preventative care, access to care, disease management, to simply understand how to best navigate a hospital campus.

Our organization is also evaluating expanding the utilization of augmented reality (avatars) to assist beyond revenue cycle to other educational situations. For example, assisting a patient and family to navigate outpatient surgery or the birth of a child. Interactive assistance with logistics, preparation, what to expect, discharge instructions, postcare assistance, etc. This has gotten a lot of wheels turning on how we can use this kind of technology to ensure better clinical outcomes, reduce readmissions and complications, and improve the Patient Financial Experience.

*Bradley Tinnermon, Vice President Revenue Cycle
and Revenue Integrity, Banner Health*

Wade: Like many of you I only came to escape, but I found something much bigger than just myself. Are you willing to fight?! Help us save the OASIS. (1)

Questions & Considerations

- How technologically advanced is your Revenue Cycle?

- What would it mean for your hospital or health system to be first to market with innovative technologies and new ways to engage with patients?

- Have you considered new technologies like Augmented Reality, Virtual Reality, and Mixed Reality?

CHAPTER 8

The New World

The dystopian nation of Panem for decades has kept the Districts under its control in varying states of poverty and required a pair of teens from each District to compete in the life-or-death Hunger Games each year. Katness Everdeen (also called Mockingjay) and her partner Peeta Mellark, winners of one of the series of Hunger Games, have successfully led a rebellion that transformed Panem into New Panem.

> **New Panem President Alma Coin:** [spreads her arms] Welcome to the New Panem. Today, on the Avenue of the Tributes, all of Panem, a free Panem, will watch more than a mere spectacle. We are gathered to witness an historic moment of justice. Today, the greatest friend to the revolution will fire the shot to end all wars. May her arrow signify the end of tyranny and the beginning of a new era. Mockingjay, may your aim be as true as your heart is pure."
> *The Hunger Games, Mockingjay 2*, Lionsgate Entertainment, 2015. (1)

The last stage of the Journey brings the hero back to The Ordinary World with skills so powerful she changes not only herself but also those around her. The hero restores balance or preserves what's good about the Ordinary World. Or, when she returns from the quest, she carries a new skill or wisdom and shares it with others to transform the ordinary into the New World.

Previous chapters in this book provide a framework for The New World of the revenue cycle. It all starts with the customer service concept of the concierge.

Concierge Services

The retail concierge market, which helps consumers get theater tickets, dining reservations, business services, housekeeping, maintenance, and personal services while they are traveling or even when they're at home in their apartments or office buildings, has grown widely and quickly. In 2013 the market totaled $1.5 billion worldwide, with 60 percent of it centered in the U.S. In 2017 the market reached $4 billion and employed nearly 128,000 people in more than 125,000 businesses. With less overall leisure time—only a little over five hours a day for most Americans—no wonder consumers are turning to concierges to handle many of the things they don't have time for. (2–3)

Healthcare Concierges

It shouldn't come as a surprise that in the last few years the concierge has moved into healthcare. According to a survey of twenty thousand physicians, done on behalf of The Physicians Foundation, 20 percent of doctors are currently practicing concierge medicine or they plan to do so in the near future. (4)

Concierge healthcare networks typically charge patients an out-of-pocket yearly fee to gain full access to specialized services or a team of primary care physician members. The networks follow one of four service models:

- Travel medical assistance, which helps travelers with emergency care as well as foreign physicians and hospitals while they're on the road
- Private health advisories, which offer services over and above standard primary care, including individualized physical examinations, direct links for second opinions, and day-to-day management of complex chronic diseases
- A private physician practice, which provides house calls, quick response to a patient's question, and a high level of personal contact and interaction
- The total care platform, which includes all of the above plus customized medical contingency plans, immediate emergency diagnosis and treatment plus routine electronic monitoring. The platform relies heavily on technology—monitors to track vital signs and smartphones to send clinical information back and forth between patient and physician, change prescriptions and treatment plans electronically, and manage virtual chronic disease clinics. (5)

Some hospitals are following a similar path to reap the benefits that concierge networks are bringing to primary care physicians: more stability in a rapidly changing healthcare climate; improved profit margins; better control over the process and delivery of healthcare; and higher patient satisfaction. Once considered a service only the rich could afford, concierge healthcare is gaining in popularity among patients in lower income brackets, and it's part of an overall brand of success.

Of the top four hospitals in *U.S. News and World Report's* 2017 rankings, all had some type of concierge service. For patients who pay for the concierge network, Mayo Clinic provides free lodging and transportation for out-of-town patients. In addition to a travel health service, Cleveland Clinic streamlines accessibility, lengthens appointment times, and enhances communication with physicians as well as a coordinated healthcare team for patients in its Florida concierge network. Johns Hopkins connects patients outside the state of Maryland with hospital physicians who provide specialized services. Massachusetts General Hospital sends patients to one of three designated primary care physicians, personalized nutritional and wellness counselors, and surgeons or other specialized practitioners. (6)

Other hospitals are expected to add concierge medical programs of their own to keep increasingly tech-savvy patients who are used to electronic interactions and increase the patient population base they might otherwise lose.

What would a concierge mean for the Patient Financial Experience? It could be just the kind of mind-set for addressing some of the most difficult problems haunting The Ordinary World of today's revenue cycle.

A Concierge for the Patient Financial Experience

Let's pause a minute and consider what people think about a concierge. To most, a concierge is someone who'll go the extra mile to give great service and provide what you need at the moment you need it most. There's an element of luxury associated with a concierge, sure. A great concierge is somehow able, through know-how, the power of persuasion, contacts, and communication skills, to score great seats for a sold-out Broadway show or get transport to the airport in the pouring rain when all cabs in the area are full. But, in the end, the concierge is all about high-quality customer service.

Concierges are best known for:

1. Making things easier for travelers. According to the online source of information about the hospitality industry, Best Hospitality Degrees, concierges frequently serve as personal assistants as well as private or for-hire chauffeurs to arrange tours and excursions or transfer passengers to and from airports, and provide perks such as the morning newspaper or latte.

2. Improving hospitality. Hotel concierges are considered the standard for hospitality today, providing a range of services from theater and dinner reservations, initial check-in, and fulfilling requests. They often are the first point of contact for hotel guests and have ongoing contact throughout the stay.

3. Assisting visitors. "In hospitals and other large-scale healthcare facilities," says Best Hospital Degrees, "concierges routinely handle the front-end tasks associated with patient occupancy and family member visitation. Hospital concierges may schedule overnight occupancy for a patient's loved ones, pass on treatment requests from relatives to nurses and care teams, and provision specific amenities prior to patient stays. Many also provide on-demand services, such as fulfilling special dietary requests or securing entertainment. A healthcare concierge could even be responsible for high-level resource management and planning. Some have been known to oversee construction and administer improvement projects, like upgrading habitability features."

4. Keeping patrons informed. No matter where they work, concierges are the go-to people for answers to questions and issues that can affect the quality of a person's stay.

5. Guest services. Greeting guests, overseeing daily operations, and keeping things running smoothly. (8)

And what if patients want a financial concierge? According to our Bridging the Gap survey they do:

- Fifty percent of patients want more help throughout the payment process
- Fifty-one percent believe having a dedicated support person to guide them through the payment process would improve their satisfaction
- Fifty percent of patients want their financial guidance to come through a concierge

But they're not finding what they want. The survey showed that:

- Fifty-five percent of patients are less than satisfied with their hospital's ability to provide the kind of financial service they desire
- While 66 percent of patients rate revenue cycle staff positively in terms of professionalism and friendliness, 35 percent are not satisfied with the clarity of the information they receive.

Providers are aware of this. Nearly all (93 percent) of the providers in the survey said a concierge service would improve the Patient Financial Experience. (9)

So how would a concierge concept translate to the healthcare financial setting? It's not as difficult a transition as you might think. Patients have the same kinds of needs that hotel guests do: information and help with logistics. So, for instance, the initial encounter at a hotel or hospital would essentially be the same and involve a warm greeting, addressing the person by name and asking how they may be of assistance, a conversation about a problem or concern, and a discussion of the options that are available.

Going the extra mile and getting tickets to the show that has been sold out for three years is grist for the hotel concierge mill. For the revenue cycle concierge? It may involve fully screening the patient for charity care eligibility or carefully analyzing the patient's current coverage and how it applies to follow-up care going forward, or offering a no-interest payment plan to cover a higher-than-expected out-of-pocket balance.

Whether hotel guest or hospital patient, both value the concierge and welcome what he or she offers because they're in the same boat: they're in unfamiliar waters and could use some navigation. Admittedly, the traditional revenue cycle has neither the investment nor the expertise today to fulfill a concierge role. But change is underway. Providers are recognizing the importance of a positive Patient Financial Experience and the elements of customer service that come into play. Let's consider a few:

PERSONALIZING PATIENT INTERACTIONS

Neither hotel concierges nor hospital revenue cycle representatives can possibly achieve positive outcomes if they don't have enough information to fulfill requests or get their jobs done. Both can be dealing with individuals who are under stress. For the hotel guest that can mean a delayed flight—again—a business presentation that has to be pulled together at the last minute, a forgotten prescription that must be filled.

For the patient it can mean health or financial concerns. One patient may be recovering from major surgery or facing a poor prognosis and more medical issues. She may have just gotten laid off, lost insurance coverage, had "low-cost" insurance that has turned out to be very expensive, or never had insurance at all. Another may have great credit and a record of always paying bills on time. This time, though, she's not sure how she can come up with the amount that's due. Still another may be eager to pay the out-of-pocket account in full—all he needs is a heads-up on the amount of the balance that will be due.

A run-of-the-mill price estimate won't do for any of them. After all, a price estimate promises to answer the question: "How much will I owe?" Giving a price quote without explanation is like leaving a homeowner who's looking for a house painter only one option: here's the price—take it or leave it. It doesn't let the homeowner comparison shop for price or scope of service.

A price estimate for a patient shouldn't be a piece of paper with numbers on it. That's not answering the real question the patient is asking. Instead of just quoting a price with little or no explanation, the provider can act as concierge. Well-trained, friendly staff can do their homework, dive into the details of the patient's coverage, and provide a really informed price estimate.

Financial Educator

This is where the revenue cycle takes on the role of financial educator. Given the complexity of healthcare coverage, even a co-pay for diagnostic tests can require some education. A patient's liability for a surgical procedure; exponentially more complex. Specialized training for the revenue cycle staff makes the difference. The saying, "It's not what you say—it's how you say it," comes to mind. A friendly demeanor, pleasant tone of voice, and frequent eye contact get the patient financial concierge off to a good start. But the revenue cycle employee also has to do some homework ahead of time and know the patient's financial situation. That means not just verifying eligibility, but also ferreting out potential issues such as out-of-network status, coverage limitations, exclusions, payer timeframe requirements for authorization, and so much more. It is the behind-the-scenes work so when it comes time to have the financial conversation with a patient, the revenue cycle hero is "on stage" and the numbers are seamless and solid.

TAILORING FINANCIAL SERVICES FOR THE PATIENT

There's no question the average patient is at least somewhat confused about coverage and liability, and with good reason. Think of all the different health plans in your geographical area, ranging from Medicare Advantage plans, PPOs, private fee-for-service plans, or high-deductible plans which may, or may not, be linked to health savings accounts. Consider how challenging it is to keep staff up to speed on all of these plans and their ever-changing requirements. Most revenue cycle staff will struggle occasionally with how to interpret eligibility and how it affects what the patient will owe. And these are people who deal with the ins and outs of insurance on a daily basis.

Now consider the patient's perspective. Some have never had healthcare coverage before. This could literally be the first time a patient has ever used insurance. A patient who's had insurance for years? Odds are he has a different insurance plan than the one that covered a previous healthcare encounter or a plan that's changed in some way. Is it any wonder patients come to the revenue cycle with questions?

Options. What patients don't want is a brief exchange of information. They want options. Think of a hotel guest who's looking for a dining recommendation for a special night out and wants to avoid the restaurant she tried on her last visit to town and disliked. What if she heard the concierge say: "Well, that's the restaurant I was going to send you to. I already told you that. I don't know what more I can possibly do for you."

A concierge who offers only one dining option won't have his job for long. Yet providers often respond to patients' financial questions precisely in this manner—by offering only one option.

What would a concierge approach look like in financial care? Take the example of a patient who is getting elective surgery and wants to know the cost.

A revenue cycle employee reviews what the patient's insurance will cover and the out-of-pocket costs and comes up with a price estimate that is much higher than the patient expected. There are three options for three different patients:

- An upfront deposit that meets the patient's budget and an interest-free payment plan for the balance
- Three payment installments that can be resolved before the patient begins a costly home improvement project later in the year
- Payment in full so the patient can take advantage of a prompt pay discount

The revenue cycle employee can drive satisfaction as well as payment by offering information and assistance. For a patient who all of a sudden is facing a ten thousand dollar bill for surgery, having a manageable payment plan before she has to schedule the procedure will give her one less thing to worry about. And her "good news story" will do more than just resolve an account—it will redefine the revenue cycle as a department that pays attention not only to the bottom line, but also the hospital's mission of providing attentive and compassionate healthcare.

BUILDING TRUST

There are many reasons to update and transform the Patient Financial Experience but none more important than building trust with patients.

Interestingly, we've found that almost half of the patients who pay their outstanding balances still call in to the revenue cycle office with questions. Why don't patients who intended to pay in the first place simply go to the payment portal or mail in a payment when they receive the bill? One reason is they don't trust the bill or the process that led up to it because they have questions about their insurance, the charges, their deductible status, or other issues and the questions need answers. Also interesting: roughly 20 percent of patients who do NOT pay, call in to the revenue cycle, adding time and cost to the collection process, because they have questions that are not being answered to their satisfaction. (10)

Patients don't have trust when financial discussions do not fully explain the ins and outs of the healthcare bill, when there's no explanation of the why behind the amount that's due.

The concierge approach can address these informational and service-oriented issues. Complete, accurate, and understandable information, combined with customer-service skills, is a winning combination for a provider. Trust begins at the very start of the financial conservation with patients and it builds at every touch point from that time on.

PREVENTING PROBLEMS/TROUBLESHOOTING

Personalizing and tailoring the financial experience to each patient also helps avoid problems. Let's take a look at two examples:

For scheduled patients: During preregistration, revenue cycle staff gather demographic and insurance information but do not discuss patient specifics so at the end of the encounter, the patient knows no more about the financial situation than before. A surprise medical bill, and all the associated dissatisfaction it entails, are inevitable.

Imagine a patient financial concierge who takes the patient step-by-step through her existing healthcare coverage and obligations and offers financing options ahead of time. Not only no surprises later on, but also a commitment to pay, and a satisfied patient.

For ER patients: While waiting for care in the hospital emergency room, a patient is never told that he will have to pay for the visit or what the amount will be. Again, a surprise bill—and of course, dissatisfaction. Asking for payment seems improper and inappropriate when a patient is sick enough to need emergency examination and possible treatment. It also can lead to complaints or regulatory issues. But some brief financial education by a patient financial concierge makes sure the ER patient understands the financial liability so he is prepared for payment down the line.

Consistency is particularly important. Because payer requirements, and the patient's insurance plan may change, or additional services may be provided, there's often a need for revenue cycle staff to revisit financial conversations with patients. Just as service-oriented companies are there for consumers when an issue arises at some point in time, the same needs to be true of the revenue cycle: The provider is always there for the patient, to handle the patient's clinical needs and the financial ones as well. If an unexpected financial issue comes up, the provider is reachable, approachable, and will work with the patient to handle it.

SETTING THE STAGE FOR SATISFACTION

The clinical world follows a shared decision-making model so the clinician and the patient make decisions together. Clinicians do their best to inform the patient of the risks and benefits of treatment, and the educated patient participates in the process. Ultimately, a personalized treatment plan is decided on.

Financial care should be treated the same way. Revenue cycle employees should explain financial "risks and benefits" so patients can make good decisions, and patients must be very clear that they expect this kind of help from hospitals.

Remember, when revenue cycle staff offer patients personalized financing options, they're viewed differently by all involved parties:

Patients view revenue cycle staff as resources. These are people the patient actively seeks out, and they become part of the story of good financial care.

Revenue cycle employees themselves have a new mind-set about the work they do. They're finding ways to help patients get the healthcare they need without undue financial burden. It's no coincidence that morale and retention tend to improve when revenue cycle employees take on the concierge role.

Hospital leaders see the connection between great financial care and wider profit margins.

A recent study by The Beryl Institute took a deeper look at the elements that are most important to patients in their healthcare experience. The survey of two thousand people in five countries, across four continents, found that six out of ten respondents identified the patient experience as important as they defined it. Above all else, the individuals in this survey wanted to be "communicated with in a way they could understand" and to be "treated with dignity and respect." Jason A. Wolf, editor of the *Patient Experience Journal*, which is published in association with The Beryl Institute, concluded that the research reinforces the view that the patient experience is a differentiator for healthcare now and in the future.

"That experience is not about being nice or making people happy," he wrote. Nor is it "a fad that will come and go. Rather, it is all about a commitment to the human experience, to engaging the person in front of you, be they patient or family member or team member or colleague." (11)

In healthcare, as well as retail and entertainment, people want—and they are coming to expect—a top-level experience overall. That is their New World—and the New World of the revenue cycle.

Peeta Mellark: Katniss, when I see you again, it will be a different world. (1)

CHAPTER 9

The End of the Journey

It's easy to blame high-dollar, out-of-pocket liability for rising patient dissatisfaction, but I've come to realize the actual amount owed is only part of the picture here. More to the point are problems in the revenue cycle: ineffective training, late financial conversations, lack of patient education regarding their health plan benefits or overall financial responsibility. These problems are adding to the volume of slow patient payments, increasing bad debt, sabotaging patient loyalty and increasing the cost to collect. It's time to stop the destruction inflicted on providers by these villains of the revenue cycle. Other industries are evolving and expanding their vision as it relates to customer satisfaction. Providers need to implement change, too, by investing in the Patient Financial Experience to gain satisfied patients and healthier margins.

All of us in healthcare know providers, in general, are notoriously slow to change. The Patient Financial Experience is unfortunately no exception. Hospital leaders talk a lot about it; yet when it comes to committing resources to change it for the better, it's more of a piecemeal approach. Maybe a provider invests in a new payment portal, but the results are disappointing because patients get one piece of the financial care they need, but not others. Even the greatest payment portal is of no use to a patient who has a complex set of questions.

And what good is a simplified bill that's great to look at, if the patient doesn't trust the amount? The same is true of cost to collect—if outdated models don't take into account whether payments require assistance, they hurt the hospital financially. Likewise, if revenue cycle employees who interact with patients are poorly trained, they can do little to prevent escalation and complaints. Without data on how satisfied patients are with their financial experience, providers don't know where they are, how they perform over time, or how to make strategic changes.

Timing is critical here. Hospitals are losing market share, margins are narrowing, and healthcare consumerism is marching on. All trends are pointing to the need for change. We know that if hospitals spend money to improve financial care, they'll ultimately collect more, they'll collect earlier, and patients will be happier. Fewer accounts will go to bad debt and cost less to collect. But without focus and investment, change can't happen. Financial care is stagnant—never a good place for hospitals to be.

When it comes to financial care, it's time for providers to bridge the gap with their patients. One of the biggest discrepancies we found in our survey was the difference in attitude between providers and patients about the money conversation. Patients want financial discussions early on, but too often, they don't happen until weeks or even months after the care episode. Outdated processes are one problem, but it's the mind-set that's the real barrier here. There's a perception in healthcare that patients will be offended if providers talk about money. We often hear that patient access departments struggle with "reluctant collectors"—staff who just don't feel comfortable asking patients for payment, so they don't. And the "reluctant collector" attitude is often present at the highest levels of the hospital. Some board members feel the same as front-end employees—that somehow it's contrary to the hospital's mission to ask patients for payment. Of course, hospitals don't have the option of taking money out of the equation if they want to continue to serve the community. And patients deserve to know their out-of-pocket costs upfront. I believe this discomfort around the financial aspect of healthcare hinders efforts to invest in the Patient Financial Experience.

While decisions about investing in the components of good financial care aren't easy for leadership to get excited about, providers are investing significant resources in the Patient Experience. It's become a top organizational priority with very good reason. Yet the same priority is not given to the financial side of the patient's hospital experience, even though it's the first, and the last, point of interaction between patients and providers. It can be a blind spot for hospital decision makers who don't put financial experiences on the same par as clinical experiences. Because, in reality, patients do not separate the clinical from the financial experiences at the hospital. For patients, all aspects of the hospital experience—clinical, financial, or otherwise—determine their overall satisfaction.

The Patient Financial Experience is not just a nice add-on to overall patient satisfaction metrics. In fact, it's clearly become a powerful differentiator for consumers. It can be the trigger of dissatisfaction that sets off a domino effect of financial disasters at your hospital. Or it can be the "X factor" that drives patients to your hospital in record numbers, widening those super tight margins to a healthy level.

After many years in the industry, I've come to an important realization about healthcare today. People are getting increasingly intolerant of outdated hospital financial practices. Patients want a healthcare financial experience that's comparable to a high-end retail experience, as our recent market study showed. Patients are clear. They want:

- a lot of information and early on, with plenty of options, a simpler bill, knowledgeable employees; and
- a "concierge" financial encounter to help them resolve their liability.

None of this is pie-in-the-sky, and none of it is rocket science. It requires an investment and a commitment to get it right, to get beyond the discussion phase, and choose to invest in modern financial care, just as hospitals invest in modern clinical care. If a hospital's surgery center was terribly outmoded, the board would greenlight an investment in a state-of-the-art center in a minute. Well, the financial services side of healthcare is terribly outmoded and can lead a hospital to financial distress. The same urgency is needed to update the financial care that's being provided by hospitals.

If this book accomplishes one thing, I'd like it to be that you start thinking about the financial experience in that way. Imagine your hospital being the one patients compare all their future healthcare financial experiences to. It's time to put on that superhero cape and start the Hero's Journey.

References and Resources

Chapter One

1. https://www.the-numbers.com/box-office-records/
worldwide/all-movies/creative-types/super-hero

2. https://www.statista.com/statistics/589978/harry-potter-
book-sales/

3. https://www.publishersweekly.com/pw/by-topic/childrens/
childrens-industry-news/article/56411-hunger-games-still-
rules-in-children-s-facts-figures-2012.html

4. http://vgsales.wikia.com/wiki/Tomb_Raider

5. https://www.britannica.com/biography/Joseph-Campbell-
American-author

6. Campbell J: The Hero with a Thousand Faces, Pantheon
Books, 1949

7. https://billmoyers.com/content/ep-1-joseph-campbell-and-
the-power-of-myth-the-hero%E2%80%99s-adventure-
audio/

8. http://www.movieoutline.com/articles/the-hero-journey-mythic-structure-of-joseph-campbell-monomyth.html

9. https://www.nyfa.edu/student-resources/5-films-that-play-out-the-monomyth/

10. https://www.forbes.com/search/?q=david%20wilkins #325a8bfb279f

11. Walker S: *The Captain Class*, Penguin Books, 2017

12. Fussell C: *One Mission*, Penguin Books, 2017

13. Draper T: *The Startup Hero*, 2017

14. Satell G: *Mapping Innovation*, McGraw-Hill, 2017

15. https://www.predictablesuccess.com/about/

16. Kaufman E: *Leadership as a Hero's Journey*, Ben Davis Press, La Mesa, CA, 2013

17. https://cramerinstitute.com/

Chapter Two

1. https://www.imdb.com/title/tt0119654/

2. https://www.jpmorganchase.com/corporate/institute/report-affording-healthcare.htm

3. Kaiser Family Foundation 2016, Sep 14

4. Wiik J: *The Patient Is the New Payer*; McKinsey & Co., from *The Patient Is the New Payer*

5. Advisory Board, 2015, from *The Patient Is the New Payer*

6. Connance, Becker's CFO Report, 2016

7. https://www.healthfirstfinancial.com/2017/09/05/patient-satisfaction-billing/

8. Avadyne: Bridging the Gap

9. American Hospital Association: Uncompensated Hospital Care Cost Fact Sheet, Dec. 2017

10. Moodys, 2018 AHA Chartbook from: Daly R: *What's Driving Increased Hospital Cost Concerns*, HFMA, July 13, 2018

11. Lazerow R: What 146 C-suite executives told us about their top concerns—and how they've changed this year, Advisory Board, July 11, 2018

12. Wiik J: CFOs and Revenue Cycle Leaders are seeking new ways to improve performance without making costly investments. HFMA: 2015 CFO survey

13. https://www.aha.org/system/files/2018-07/2018-aha-chartbook.pdf

14. https://www.advisory.com/

15. https://www.kaufmanhall.com/sites/default/files/2017-State-of-Cost-Transformation-in-U.S.-Hospitals.pdf

Chapter Three

1. https://www.imdb.com/title/tt0133093/quotes

2. Vogler C: *The Writer's Journey*. Michael West Productions, Studio City, CA, 2007

3. Avadyne Health: Bridging the Gap, 2018

4. https://physiciansfoundation.org/research-insights/biennial-physician-surveys-patient-surveys/

5. https://www.tennessean.com/story/money/industries/health-care/2016/03/07/why-more-than-half-hospital-bills-dont-get-paid/81297202/

Chapter Four

1. https://www.imdb.com/title/tt1825683/quotes

2. https://www.cms.gov/Medicare/Quality-Initiatives-Patient-Assessment-Instru-ments/HospitalQualityInits/HospitalHCAHPS.html

3. Avadyne Health: Bridging the Gap

4. file:///C:/Users/owner/Downloads/HBI-%20Clinical%20Intelligence%20in%20Rev%20Cycle-WP_55A1FB11-CA79-49FC-6B342D08736A689A11.pdf

Chapter Five

1. https://www.imdb.com/title/tt1790864/quotes

2. http://www.hfma.org/Content.aspx?id=30965

3. https://www.cnbc.com/2017/06/26/two-in-three-patients-cant-pay-off-their-hospital-bills.html

4. https://www.beckershospitalreview.com/finance/patient-engagement-in-the-out-of-pocket-era.html

5. https://www.theatlantic.com/business/archive/2017/06/medical-bills/530679/

6. Wiik: *The Patient Is the New Payer*

7. https://www.healthcarebusinessinsights.com/blog/patient-financial-experience/defining-measuring-patient-financial-experience/

8. Avadyne Health: internal information

9. Avadyne Health: Bridging the Gap

10. https://www.aha.org/system/files/research/reports/tw/chartbook/2016/2016chartbook.pdf

11. Avadyne Health

12. www.experian.com/healthconsumerstudy

13. https://www.kvue.com/article/news/investigations/defenders/medical-billing-complaints-escalate/212345325

14. https://cdn2.hubspot.net/hubfs/402746/Assets/West%20Assets/Prioritizing%20the%20Patient%20Experience/Patient%20Exp%20Handout_Final-1.pdf?t=1497642504805

15. Int J Health Care Qual Assur. 2011;24(4):266–73

16. https://www2.deloitte.com/us/en/pages/life-sciences-and-health-care/articles/hospitals-patient-experience.html

17. https://www.medirevv.com/blog/how-speech-analytics-technology-enhances-the-patient-financial-experience

18. Vogler, *The Writer's Journey*

19. https://scatteredquotes.com/10-best-maze-runner-scorch-trials-quotes-2015/

Chapter Six

1. https://www.imdb.com/title/tt0451279/quotes

2. Sources: Solomon M: Thanks a LATTE: How to Fix a Customer Service Failure, per Starbucks, Marriott and me. *Forbes Magazine* Nov 19, 2017

3. Solomon M: The Secrets of Customer Service Recovery, Nextiva, 2017

4. HFMA

5. https://news.gallup.com/poll/225383/uninsured-rate-steady-fourth-quarter-2017.aspx

6. https://www.advisory.com/topics/finance/revenue-cycle/billing-and-collections

7. http://healthcare.mckinsey.com/sites/default/files/762679_US_healthcare_payments_Remedies_for_an_ailing_system.pdf

8. http://healthcare.mckinsey.com/sites/default/files/762679_US_healthcare_payments_Remedies_for_an_ailing_system.pdf

9. https://www.healthcareitnews.com/news/revenue-cycle-management-vendors-ranked-black-book

10. http://www.pewinternet.org/fact-sheet/social-media/

11. Avadyne Health, internal research

12. https://www.imdb.com/title/tt0451279/quotes

Chapter Seven

1. https://www.imdb.com/title/tt1677720/quotes

2. Augmented Reality in the Real World, *Harvard Business Review*, November–December 2017

3. http://www.digitalmeetsculture.net/article/ikea-launches-augmented-reality-app-lets-you-preview-digital-furniture-in-your-physical-house/

4. https://www.pcmag.com/news/363090/the-future-of-augmented-reality-is-serious-business

5. https://www.marketsandmarkets.com/PressReleases/augmented-reality.asp

6. https://sciencebasedmedicine.org/augmented-reality-in-medicine/

7. https://medicalfuturist.com/augmented-reality-in-healthcare-will-be-revolutionary

8. https://www.prnewswire.com/news-releases/healthcares-digital-divide-widens-black-book-consumer-survey-300384816.html

Chapter Eight

1. https://www.imdb.com/title/tt1951266/quotes

2. https://www.ibisworld.com/industry-trends/specialized-market-research-reports/advisory-financial-services/other-outsourced-functions/business-concierge-services.html

3. https://fivethirtyeight.com/features/heres-how-americans-spend-their-working-relaxing-and-parenting-time/

4. https://www.merritthawkins.com/news-and-insights/blog/healthcare-news-trends/who-will-embrace-concierge-medicine/

5. https://www.forbes.com/sites/russalanprince/2013/05/30/what-is-concierge-healthcare/#78d826e75c6d

6. http://www.modernhealthcare.com/article/20171021/NEWS/171019863

7. https://www.besthospitalitydegrees.com/faq/what-exactly-is-the-hospitality-industry/

8. Avadyne Health, Bridging the Gap

9. Avadyne Health, internal research

10. Wolf Jason: *The Consumer Has Spoken, Patient Experience Journal*, vol 5, issue 1, 2018

About the Author

With more than twenty-five years of experience in the business of hospitals and health systems, Jayson Yardley, CEO, innovator, entrepreneur, and speaker shares his insights about the changing consumerism in healthcare and the bold and disruptive strategies needed to transform the patient financial experience. During his career, which began behind an emergency room desk admitting patients, transitioned to a decade in consulting, and expanded to CEO/President of multiple revenue cycle management companies, Jayson has encountered many revenue cycle and healthcare heroes and hopes *Rev Up!* empowers all to take flight and achieve new heights of success and courageous transformation.